Skiing is my Passion

Tommy

About My Story

When I first started writing my story in November 2012, my mom's health was deteriorating rapidly. She always wanted me to write a book about my ski career, yet in the same breath she would say, "But then again you never read a book!"

Being dyslexic and growing up not knowing how to read and process words made me focus more on what I could do... SPORTS! I was very athletic, but my passion was skiing which began in Aspen in 1955.

Without an athletic program in high school, I wouldn't have made it. I barely graduated, wasn't smart enough to get into college, and my choices were the Vietnam War, or take a chance and pursue a ski career. I chose the latter!

After two years' internship in California, failing my draft physical, receiving full Certification status and careful consideration, I moved to Aspen permanently in 1970.

Choosing a career in skiing presents a problem, unless you are willing to follow

Snowmass 2014. Courtesy of Tracy Shopkorn

winter. I wasn't! I had to use all the resources I had in the winter to survive the summers.

This story is a resume of my journey to do just that. Ski, live, work and play in Aspen, Colorado.

My career in Aspen spanned four plus decades. I feel blessed to have watched this little mining town evolve from, "Dogs, Dirt and Dope" in the Seventies; to "Sex, Drugs and Rock & Roll" in the eighties and nineties; to today's real estate Mecca, which introduced, "The Rich, the Rude and the Greedy". Changes are inevitable, whether it's technology, money, power or politics. But the one thing you can't change is the free spirited attitude and the beauty of this valley which will keep attracting people forever.

I hope you enjoy reading my story as much as I enjoyed living it.

The names remain unchanged as my intentions are not to hurt anyone. If I put a little extra jam on the bread, so be it! It's my story...

Courtesy Fallon Feast Buttermilk 2014

"It's the journey, not the destination!"

World Record for Health, Aspen Mountain 2000. Photo courtesy Chris Hanson

GUINNESS® WORLD RECORDS

CERTIFICATE

TOMMY WALTNER
COMPLETED A WORLD RECORD
23 FRONT INVERTED AERIAL
JUMPS WITHIN 10 MINUTES ON
ASPEN MOUNTAIN, COLORADO, USA,
IN ORDER TO RAISE MONEY FOR
TOMMY'S 'LOOPS FOR LUPUS' CAMPAIGN
ON 25 APRIL 2000

Keeper of the Records
GUINNESS WORLD RECORDS LTD

United States Patent [19]

Waltner

[11] Patent Number: **Des. 332,546**

[45] Date of Patent: ** Jan. 19, 1993

[54] **COMBINED STADIUM BAG AND SEAT**

[76] Inventor: **Thomas E. Waltner**, 999 Garfield, Carbondale, Colo. 81623

[**] Term: **14 Years**

[21] Appl. No.: **389,102**

[22] Filed: **Aug. 3, 1989**

[52] U.S. Cl. **D6/601**; D6/502

[58] Field of Search D6/491, 500–503, D6/509–511, 595–596, 601, 604; 5/420, 481

[56] **References Cited**

U.S. PATENT DOCUMENTS

D. 283,771	5/1986	Howard	D6/596
D. 293,282	12/1987	Ashford	D6/502 X
D. 306,543	3/1990	Pestuglicci et al.	D6/601
D. 308,454	6/1990	Merli	D6/596
D. 312,741	12/1990	Treadwell	D6/601
2,868,274	1/1959	Miller	D6/502 X
4,597,605	7/1986	Gilbert	D6/601 X
4,843,662	7/1989	Handelman	D6/601 X
4,863,003	9/1989	Carter	5/420 X

Primary Examiner—Nelson C. Holtje
Assistant Examiner—Janice E. Seeger
Attorney, Agent, or Firm—Kyle W. Rost

[57] **CLAIM**

The ornamental design for a combined stadium bag and seat, as shown and described.

DESCRIPTION

FIG. 1 is a top plan view of a combined stadium bag and seat, showing my new design; the bottom being a mirror image thereof;

FIG. 2 is a left side elevational view thereof;

FIG. 3 is a right side elevational view thereof;

FIG. 4 is an end elevational view thereof;

FIG. 5 is an elevational view, showing the end not shown in FIG. 4; and,

FIG. 6 is a top plan view showing the combined stadium bag and seat in open position.

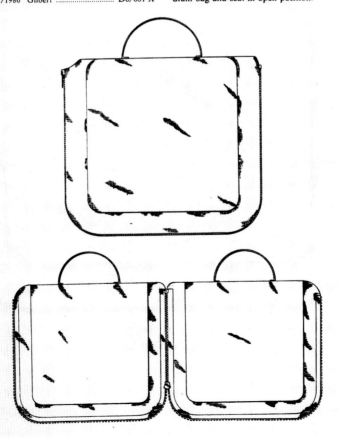

The United States of America

The Commissioner of Patents and Trademarks

Has received an application for a new, original, and ornamental design for an article of manufacture. The title and description of the design are enclosed. The requirements of law have been complied with, and it has been determined that a patent on the design shall be granted under the law.

Therefore, this

United States Patent

Grants to the person or persons having title to this patent the right to exclude others from making, using or selling the design throughout the United States of America for the term of fourteen years from the date of this patent.

Acting Commissioner of Patents and Trademarks

Attest

KERMA.

High Performance Poles for High Performance People.

Distributed by Rossignol.

Copper Mountain. Photo courtesy of John Russell

FOR YOUR BEST

3 OF OUR BEST.
ROSSIGNOL
The name means performance.

Circa 1977. Photo courtesy of John Russell

July 18, 1977 / $1.00

Newsweek
Life Outdoors

Hunter Creek, Aspen, Colorado. Photo courtesy of John Russell

by Aspen's World Record Holder

Tommy Waltner

T.W.E. PUBLISHING
Tommy Waltner
Basalt, Colorado
tommy@skiingismypassion.com

Published by T.W.E. Publishing
Tommy Waltner
231 Robinson St., Loft 304
Basalt, Colorado 81621
tommy@skiingismypassion.com

ISBN 978-0-578-15736-8 paperback
ISBN ebook
Library of Congress Control Number: 2015903449

Cover & Inside Back Cover Photographs by John Russell
Back Cover & Content Page Photographs by Stephanie Manone

Cover Design by Basalt Printing
Book Design by Basalt Printing

Printed in Korea by Four Colour Print Group, Louisville, Kentucky

Jean Walzner, Ski Broadmoor, Circa 1960

*To my mom, who never
stopped believing in me even
though I didn't read.*

To Ed Bradley, who taught me more than I even taught him.

Contents

Early Years, If I Could Do It, So Can You! Fifties & Sixties 1

Off To Southern California 5

Junior High School, Surfing 7th Grade 9

Cabo San Lucas 8th Grade 12

Surfing Accident, Dyslexia 9th Grade 14

High School Athletics, Mini 10th Grade 17

Sports, Surfing and Skiing 11th Grade 22

Graduation, Porsche 12th Grade 25

Off to June Lake November 1968 29

Seventies 43

Dogs, Dirt, and Dope Winter 1969-1970 45

Wild Bird, Gun and Hashish Winter 1970-1971 49

Kathy Winter 1971-1972 60

Pepsi and Aspen Villa Winter 1972-1973 64

Michael and Rusty Winter 1973-1974 66

Mountain Dew Summer 1974 68

Ski Racing and a Really Good Songwriter Winter 1974-1975 71

Spoony's Lunch Wagon Summer 1975 74

Rossignol Consultant Winter 1975-1976 77

Grand Canyon Summer 1976 79

Rossignol Technical Representative Winter 1976-1977 82

Sea of Cortez Summer 1977 83

Michael Landon's Double Winter 1977-1978 85

Whale Sharks Summer 1978 87

Rossignol Promo Film Winter 1978-1979 88

Eighties & Nineties 91

Winter Olympics Lake Placid Winter 1979-1980 93

Kentucky Derby Summer 1980 94

Cheryl Ladd and Oil Shale Winter 1980-1981 95

Dusty Rose Restaurant and Bar Winter 1981-1982 100

Back to Skiing Winter 1982-1983 101

Ed Bradley Winter 1983-1984 103

Sold Dusty Rose Summer 1984 105

Ed and Mont Tremblant Winter 1984-1985 107

Dental Assistant Summer 1985 108

New Clients Winter 1985-1986 110

Contents

Coca-Cola and the Dental Assistant Summer 1986 110
Silver Queen Gondola Winter 1986-1987 112
Back Surgery and the Backpack Summer 1987 116
Rosie O'Grady's Flying Circus Winter 1987/1988 117
Golf Summer 1988 120
Ed and Irving Winter 1988-1989 122
LA Dodgers and Cush 'N' Carry Summer 1989 122
Sailing and Golf 1989-1990 126
Earthquake 1991 128
Cool-Apse 1993 129
Ruedi House 1994 131
Joanie and I Get Married 1996 133
Millennium And Beyond, 2000 Plus 15 .... **135**
Loops for Lupus 1999 137
World Record for Health 2000-2001 143
Ed and Bonnie's at 11:30 A.M. 2002 146
Rapid Rake 2003 148
Tommy's Magic Sauces 150
My Loft 2005 153
Maxwell vs. Panda Peak Winter 2006 155
Ed Passes 2006 158
Reflecting 161
Remembering Ed Bradley 2007 164
Chrysler Corporation 166
Age and Como 2008 167
Ed's Bench and Snowboarding 2009-2010 170
TIAs and Motorcycle Accident Winter 2011 174
EEGs and Alcohol 2012 175
Mom Passes 176
Retirement 177
Dr. Rippy 2013 177
The Accident March 2013 179
Rehab 182
Tommy's Flying Circus is Born 187
Just Fix It 189
Retrospect **190**
Acknowledgments **191**

Circa 1956

Circa 1965

Circa 1957

Circa 1961

EARLY YEARS
1950-1968

If I Could Do It, So Can You!
Fifties & Sixties

How is it possible that a person who has never read a book could write one — especially one worth reading? Despite losing my dad at age three stuttering my way through grade school, cheating my way through junior high and high school and not being able to comprehend the written word until well into my 20s. Here is my story. It begins in one of the best places for the soul of a skier to arrive on earth…Born in Colorado Springs on February 28, 1950, my father died when I was three years old. At the time of his death my older brother Bill was six and my younger sister Sandy was only a year old. My father was a World War II veteran who enjoyed hunting. He owned and operated a feed and grain store just outside of Colorado Springs. While on his way to go hunting, he died from a gunshot wound to the neck. He had placed his gun on the back seat of the car with the clip in his pocket unaware of a cartridge in the chamber. The car hit a bump and the rifle bounced off the back seat onto the floor causing a round to discharge, ricochet inside the car and land in his neck, killing him instantly.

Being a young boy at the time, I don't remember much about my dad. The few things I do remember were things that got me in trouble. I once shot him with a rubber band from a toy gun he had made for me out of a clothespin. Another time I was sitting in his lap shooting a target with a 22-caliber squirrel gun rifle. I wasn't a very good shot and I imagine he got frustrated with me.

My mom was beautiful, young, and now single. After my father passed away she raised the three of us without accepting much help from our maternal grandparents Moey and Bop. I don't think they were very happy that Mom had married our father, but our lives would have been a lot different without them. They were such a big part of our lives and always there for us. My mom was a very proud woman who worked extremely hard trying to make the

Sunday Dinner at the ranch with Moey and Bop.
Circa 1955

best life possible for us. She worked for the local newspaper, *The Gazette*, in Colorado Springs and later became a ski instructor at Ski Broadmoor.

She raised us much like all single moms did, we went to school and she went to work. I remember coming home from school each day and Moey would always be there with donuts, our "afternoon treat" as she would call it, usually leaving just as Mom would be coming home from work. We lived at the base of Cheyenne Mountain in a small area called Skyway Park. It was very close to the Broadmoor Hotel in a modest neighborhood. On Sundays we would travel to Moey and Bop's house on the outskirts of town for sit-down Sunday dinners. After dinner Bop would always take us to do something. He lived on a non-working ranch and didn't raise livestock or grow hay, most likely because he was busy working as a prominent securities broker in the Springs. Despite his busy schedule, he always had time for his grandkids, taking us fishing, exploring around the ranch or to the nearby toy store.

A year or so after our father passed away my mom dated guys from The Tenth Mountain Division and Fort Carson, an army base near the Springs. That's when we started doing lots of outdoor activities. We learned to ski in Aspen, Colorado on Aspen Mountain. I remember meeting for our ski lessons at a gazebo in a field called Paepcke Park. From there we would ride a horse drawn carriage to the ski lift at the nearby hill called The Little Nell. The ski lift was a T-bar that you would sit against as it pulled you up. I was too little to ride it like that so I would just hang on as long as I could and let it pull me up the hill about a couple of hundred yards. The next year a double chair lift was put in. At the end of the day we would ski down the street to the Hotel Jerome to meet our mom for après ski at the Jerome bar, the "J-Bar". In the evenings we usually ate at the Red Onion restaurant, located out in the middle of a field about a block or two from the gazebo in Paepcke Park.

We visited Aspen during the summers as well, driving over Independence Pass on winding dirt roads. We spent most of our winters skiing at Pikes Peak and other nearby ski areas (Loveland, Arapahoe Basin, Ski Cooper and Climax). Once Ski Broadmoor opened we spent most of our weekends there. It was close by and Mom worked there. There was also night skiing, so when I began ski racing I would train on the weekends and a couple of times a week at night, eventually becoming a pretty good ski racer finishing in the top three of my division in most of my races.

In 1960, Ski Broadmoor had lost the bid for the Olympics to Squaw Village. However, its curiosity between snowmaking and night skiing attracted skiers from all over the world. I had the opportunity to ski with Stein Eriksen, Buddy Werner and Hans Peter Lanig. Hans stayed in Colorado Springs and coached me for a year. At the end of my early ski-racing career I placed second in a four-state competition at the Rocky Mountain Ski Racers Association at Arapahoe Basin. There were hopes I'd compete in the 1968 Winter Olympics in Grenoble if I kept with it.

From the look on my face Uh Oh! comes to mind.
Pikes Peak, Circa 1956

I remember when I first took swimming lessons at six years old. Mom took my brother Bill and me to the pool at the Broadmoor Hotel. When we came out of the locker room I jumped into the pool right behind Bill. He had taken lessons the year before, but I hadn't. I almost drowned. The swimming instructor rescued me and I didn't get back into the pool until I was nine. Mom bribed me by telling me she would give me a dollar when I could jump off the diving board without a life jacket, or someone holding a pole at the side of the pool to pull me out. It worked, because by the age of ten I was competing in springboard diving competitions. The men my mom dated would take me to diving exhibitions in Denver, Fort Carson and the local YMCA. I was very impressed with this incredibly beautiful sport, but I felt I was a much better ski racer than a diver.

My mom remarried in the spring of 1961 to a wonderful man Dave Maytag, heir to the Maytag washing machine fortune. I had a wonderful childhood and was blessed to have been brought up with such a great mom, new dad and wonderful grandparents, who did so much for us. I was really looking forward to this next chapter of my life. I now had the dad I missed so much while growing up. Even so, it was difficult for Sandy, Bill, and me to call him dad so we all decided "Dave" was fine and he was totally okay with it, despite this being his first marriage. After the wedding they sat us down and asked us if it would be okay to move to California.

Dave, Mom and Dave's partner Mike celebrating victory at the Reno Air Races. Reno, Nevada, 1964

I think the first thing out of my mouth was, "Do they have snow?" We were so happy to have a dad that it didn't matter where we moved, although we did have a lot of questions.

Dave satisfied our curiosity by taking us flying in his P-51 Mustang. A few years later, that same airplane won a transcontinental race from Clearwater, Florida to Reno, Nevada in the annual Reno air show, which people from all over the world competed in. Dave also took us shopping for things we needed for our new house in southern California. Because it had a very long driveway, he felt we had to have a go-kart. We had definitely gone from rags to riches. Our prior life was hardly rags but we thought that going to a new place called "McDonald's" for a coke was spoiling us! This was going to be wild!

Off to Southern California

I had just turned 11 years old a few months earlier and the thought of leaving my grandparents, my friends, and my skiing family that I was so fond of, was kind of scary. I was up for anything with my new dad, so we loaded up in his new 1961 black Chevy Impala and off we went. Mom and Dave were in the front and Bill and I got the window seats, leaving Sandy in the middle. We told her it would be a "party foul" if we didn't sit boy, girl, boy. We drove the southern route through New Mexico, Arizona and the desert east of Los Angeles. I remember Dave telling Bill, "You're going to love it here with all the movie stars and their pretty daughters."

That didn't hold much interest for me. I wanted to see this ocean they had been telling me about back in school. The largest body of water I had ever seen was a little lake where my grandfather took me to go trout fishing.

It was about a three-day trip. For me it was amazing. The city was everywhere and it was BIG! Everything was BIG! The roads were BIG, the cars were moving fast, and the houses were BIG. As we drew closer to our new house Dave pointed out the school that Bill would attend in the fall and that was BIG! As we traveled up the road to our house we passed several homes. One was where the actor Harry Morgan lived, which didn't mean much to me at the time. Then our driveway came into view. It was very long, perfect for the go-kart. When we got to our house, it was BIG! Even better than that, it had two pools, a baby pool with a waterfall that dropped into a big pool with yes, a diving board! I had died and gone to heaven.

As we settled in Dave would take us on little sightseeing trips close to home. Our house was in Brentwood between Beverly Hills and Pacific Palisades. Santa Monica was close by and we would travel through it to get to the ocean. It was pretty cool. On a clear day you

I walked a lot because of my height. Short!
Santa Monica, 1962

could see Catalina Island twenty-six miles from the mainland. Dave kept his airplane at Santa Monica Airport. Everything was close by.

I played baseball that summer. I wasn't very big, but I was pretty gutsy, so they put me behind the plate as catcher. I played that position for a couple of years in Little League. When I was old enough to play in the Pony League the coach found a better catcher and I moved to the outfield. I was pretty fast so it worked out fine. I met a lot of friends playing ball. It seemed everyone had a pool with a diving board.

When school started that fall, Sandy and I attended Brentwood Elementary School and Bill entered ninth grade at Paul Revere Junior High, the same school that Dave had pointed out when we arrived. Junior High in California was seventh through ninth grades. I remember going into Brentwood to go school shopping. We went to this place called Bullock's Department Store. It was BIG! Mom was dragging Bill and Sandy and me through the store and suddenly they realized I was missing. Lost of course, I was crying and scared. A clerk in the store found me and announced my name in an attempt to find my mom. It worked. She found me and assured me that it would never happen again.

The main difference that year was riding a big bus to and from school. Right after school began the Bellaire fire started and our house was in danger. The principal wouldn't release us from my school without parent consent. Bill walked home from school about a mile down the road and helped Dave put sprinklers on top of the house. They threw all of the valuables in the pool including the silver and jewelry. Dave wasn't going to leave, but being concerned about Sandy and me, got the idea to hire an ambulance to pick us up at school and bring us home. The ambulance had the lights and siren running so they could get through the roadblocks along the way, and Sandy and I were told to just stay down out of sight. It worked. We made it home, but we were awake all night long. The fire was all around us and Dave was worried the authorities would force us to evacuate even though he was willing to go down with the house. Fortunately we got lucky. The fire jumped the canyon where we lived and proceeded through the Santa Monica Mountains towards Pacific Palisades and Malibu. That was a pretty tense time!

On Thanksgiving break we loaded up in Dave's new Aero Commander plane and headed back to Colorado Springs to visit our grandparents, see our friends and go skiing. We skied one more time that winter, but this time in the San Bernardino Mountains in a local place called Green Valley.

Bill and I skied the steepest part of the ski area serviced by a rope tow. Bill and I were familiar with this type of lift as Pikes Peak had several rope tows. While going up, the rope got caught in my right arm jacket sleeve and at the top I couldn't let go of the rope. It pulled me up off the ground about 10 to 15 feet to a Chevy-rim that returned the rope back to the bottom. My arm went around the rim and tore my sleeve off my jacket before the operator got the thing turned off. My brother was right behind me on the tow. He got off fine, but was laughing at me as I stood on the foot pegs straddling a pole 15 feet off the snow. As I was coming down the pole I noticed a lot of people watching me.

When the ski patrol showed up they wanted to take me down in a toboggan. It was steep and Bill and I looked at one another and decided to ski down to the patrol shack at the bottom of the hill. The patrol showed up about twenty minutes later, toboggan and all. We didn't ski any more that day. When we got home Mom and Dave drove me to UCLA Medical Hospital, where it was determined that I had broken my arm. I had to wear a cast.

I couldn't help but remember that a couple of years earlier at Pikes Peak Ski Area, a friend had a similar experience. When the rope got wet it would stretch and tighten back up when the tow leveled out. He wasn't quite as lucky as I had been, ending up being pulled headfirst into the same type of return wheel. He spent several hours in surgery having pieces of steel removed from his skull. He was okay, thank God. It reminds me how dangerous skiing could be back then.

For the rest of the school year, my neighbor and girlfriend helped me with a lot of my homework because with my cast I couldn't write. Honestly, it was a great excuse, because out on the playground everyone wanted me on their sockball team, a game similar to baseball without the bat, because my cast was like a weapon hitting the ball.

Over the course of the first school year in California I made a lot of new friends. I didn't use the swimming pool as much because I had discovered the ocean. I went to a beach club in Santa Monica with Ed and Bob: two brothers who lived down the street from me. I learned to play beach volleyball. Because I was still short and the net seemed really high to me I wasn't very good at it. They were really good and received college scholarships to UCLA. Eventually, I believe Ed made the Olympic team.

I got to know another friend Allen, who lived down the street from Ed and Bob. His mom was a movie star and drove a white Rolls Royce. She would take us to Santa Monica Pier where Allen and I fished, catching smelt, Perch, small Calico bass, and occasionally Bonita: big fighters and fun to catch. Right next to Santa Monica Pier, I discovered Pacific Ocean Park, an amusement park with a giant rollercoaster. I had been on a rollercoaster before in Colorado Springs but nothing like this one. I went there as many times as I could that summer. I still played baseball that summer and Dave really enjoyed doing that with me. I liked being a kid in California. I was always busy doing various things and I had a lot of different friends doing the same things with me. I also spent a lot of time with the girl who sat next to me and helped me in class when I broke my arm. She was pretty special. We spent time together close to home.

As summer was coming to an end, I met another neighbor Craig. One night he invited me to sleep over. My mom drove me to his house, met his mom and left me to sleep over. His house was really cool, huge like a castle. It had a movie theater and two or three different living rooms, one with ping-pong and pool tables. There was a swimming pool fenced in glass, with a high dive and a long driveway with a go-kart too. What really impressed me was a big metal disc at the top of the driveway next to the garage, with no place to turn around. When you pulled up to the garage you would pull onto this metal disc, push a button and it would turn the car around. I thought that was way cool.

As it turned out, Craig's father was an inventor who had designed the record changer for turntables. He was always down in his shop working on something. At one point, he was working on a bottle cap that could be removed without an opener. He eventually came up with a screw top for glass containers. It seemed fascinating to me to always be creating new things and I thought I would like to do that someday.

Craig and I did a lot of things together. As it turned out, his house was really close to ours. After that first night I slept over, he told me to follow him down the driveway. We walked by the pool and through the bushes until I realized we were almost standing in my front yard. I laughed, thinking about my mom. I thought it was so funny how she made such a big production of getting instructions from Craig's mom, loading up the car, driving down our driveway, up the road and up his driveway to their house. Needless to say, I walked over from then on. Craig and I continued to do a lot of things together for the next couple of years. He taught me to surf, skateboard, play football, and get in trouble like teenagers did in those days. He was my best friend.

Junior High School, Surfing
7th Grade

That year I started in a new school just a mile from where we lived. The campus was big with basketball courts, football and soccer fields. It was the seventh grade and I liked the sound of junior high school. Bill began the year in a new school as well, attending high school in Pacific Palisades and looking forward to playing football and track. I really didn't know what to expect. My new school was huge, accommodating a ton of students from other school districts. The big difference for me was the format. I had a homeroom and six classes all in different locations on campus. It was meant to prepare us for high school and then college.

I suppose like all schools, the upper class kids would mess with the new kids. I had been forewarned the summer before because all the kids I hung around with were older than I was. The upper class kids would try to sell pool passes to a non-existent pool on top of the gymnasium. I didn't fall for it, but I admit that the next year I did the same thing. It was really a way to welcome the new kids each year.

School was school: reading, writing and arithmetic. Gym class or PE as it was called, was my cup of tea. We played soccer, flag football and basketball. Basketball was my least favorite because I was short and the last to be chosen to a team. Whenever we had free PE days, I would spend my time in the outdoor gymnastic area of the playground. There were high bars, rings, rope climbing and parallel bars. I loved it, especially the high bars. I got pretty good at it, staying for hours after school. Gymnastics was offered as an elective sport, but that didn't start until the ninth grade. We did use the gym occasionally but not the gymnastics equipment.
I couldn't wait for the ninth grade.

I would go home long after the school bus had gone. I'd go to a friend's house or to the country market for a haircut, buy school supplies, or clothes, and then Mom would come and pick me up. Sometimes I would just walk home — until I discovered hitchhiking. From then on I only rode the school bus for field trips or athletic events at other schools. Unfortunately, one night during dinner I made the mistake of telling my mom and dad that I had been hitchhiking to and from school. Needless to say, I got in trouble. I didn't seem to care very much because I continued doing it, careful never to mention it again. I'm sure they knew everyone was doing it in those days.

As the holidays grew closer, Dave asked us if we wanted to go back to

Will Rodgers State Beach. Santa Monica, Circa 1963.

Without the mountains in my backyard, my love for the ocean emerged.

Colorado Springs to ski or go to Hawaii instead. That was a loaded question. Sandy, Bill and I jumped at the chance to go to Hawaii and I felt certain Mom and Dave wanted to go too. It was a great trip. I was able to perfect my surfing a bit and learn to scuba dive, which scared me, but gave me a real feel for the ocean. We went to Oahu, drove all over the island and visited all the tourist spots.

One day as we traveled around the island with one of Dave's flying buddies and his family, the fuel pump went out in our rental car. Dave and his friend, who was an engineer and inventor, rigged a glass bottle that fed the carburetor with gas by gravity. We were on the north side of the island and it worked well enough to get us back to Waikiki, where we were staying, all the way filling the bottle with gas.

Christmas came and went and once again we were spoiled with gifts. I got my first surfboard and couldn't wait to try it out the first weekend, it was nice enough to go to the beach. We also went skiing that winter. Mom arranged a week-long ski trip to Mammoth for Sandy and me between semesters in mid-January. In California the mid semesters were a big deal. Some students actually graduated in the middle of a school year, probably because there were so many students.

Summer arrived and I played a lot of baseball, surfed, skateboarded and spent a lot of time at the beach. I really enjoyed the beach and surfing was my new love. I went early before the wind would blow and the waves would get all choppy. There were enough of us that our parents or anyone old enough to drive, would take turns taking and picking us up. If we couldn't get a ride we would figure out places to stash our boards, such as a beach club or a friend's house who lived close to the beach. Then we'd hitchhike back and forth without the boards.

In those days hitchhiking was pretty safe. I don't ever remember anyone getting into trouble doing it. However, I had a couple of strange things happen to me. Once I hitchhiked into the Palisades to see a movie and was picked up by a gay person. When he placed his hand on my leg I told him, "I'll get out here." He drove me to the movie and that was that. Another time when I was 19, I was driving my Porsche up to Santa Barbara to see my grandparents. I picked up a guy in Ventura. He had a grand mal epileptic seizure and literally climbed all over the inside of my car. I pulled over and opened the passenger side door to help him out of the car. He was wearing a bracelet that said he was epileptic. That put an end to my hitchhiking experiences.

Cabo San Lucas
8th Grade

The next school year wasn't much different from the previous one, except instead of going to Hawaii for Christmas, we loaded up in Dave's Aero Commander and flew to Cabo San Lucas to a little town called Palmilla. That place was beautiful. We would get up early and meet for breakfast, get in the airplane and fly a short distance to go dove hunting. You couldn't drive anywhere in Baja, it was easier to fly. My brother and I had a ball. There were doves everywhere. I wasn't very good at shooting them and kind of scared of guns, but it was fun. Dave loved it because he had grown up bird hunting with his father. Mom liked it too. Later in life she shot clay pigeons in competitions.

We'd get enough birds, bring them back to the hotel and the staff would prepare them for dinner. We would usually be done hunting and back to the hotel by late morning. Then we'd have lunch or take it with us and meet our fishing boat to go deep-sea fishing. I loved to fish because that didn't scare me. We caught sailfish, Wahoo, and Dorado (blunt nose dolphin) and brought the Dorado back to the hotel to be prepared by the staff. Our

The love for the ocean kept growing! Palmilla, Cabo San Lucas, Baja California. Circa 1965.

fishing guide would take everything else back to his village for his people.

That winter, Mom arranged another ski trip for my sister and me with the same group we had gone with the year before. Sandy and I had skied most of our lives, so these ski trips were a lot of fun for us. It was very crowded at Mammoth and the road was closed up to the ski area due to too much snow. Instead, we took a short drive to June Lake, a small ski area just north of Mammoth. I was able to help a lot of the other kids with their skiing and I kind of felt like a

Palmilla, Cabo San Lucas
Baja California, Circa 1965

big shot. I was treated like one of the counselors — probably because I skied better than they did.

That spring was exciting for all of us. Mom and Dave had a baby girl, my half-sister Patty. It was a great time for all of us. I changed her diapers, fed her and was a good big brother. It was fun watching her grow up daily. Dave got Mom a nanny to help with my little sister, which was a relief for Mom. It had to be difficult starting another family. I'm sure Sandy, Bill and I were enough of a handful being teenagers. That summer was going to be busy with a new baby.

Dave bought a new airplane, a B-26 Bomber. It was bigger than the Commander, just like our family. Dave had a ranch in Pinedale, Wyoming that he inherited from his father. It was a large working ranch with hay, horses, cattle and great fishing. That summer Bill and Sandy both went to camp in Wyoming. Sandy went to one in Jackson Hole, 90 miles north of the ranch. Bill went to a cowboy camp in Rock Springs, 90 miles south of the ranch. I had had a bad experience at a church camp in Colorado Springs, so I didn't go to camp. Instead I got to fly to Wyoming several times that summer and fish a lot.

I also went to Catalina Island with my friend Doug, who went to school and played baseball with me. We flew over in a seaplane. I'd never been in one of those before. I sat next to a lady who also had never been in a seaplane. We started talking and she asked me if I had ever been in a small plane before and being the spoiled little brat that I was, I told her all about flying with Dave.

To make money to spend in the penny arcade, Doug and I hauled luggage in our wagons for the tourists who stayed at the Catalina hotels. We snorkeled and spear fished with Hawaiian slings, poles with spear shaped tips at one end and a big rubber band at the other. I spent most of my time snorkeling, hauling luggage and spending the money I earned at the penny arcade. I sure loved Catalina. When I returned to the mainland Mom took me directly to the hospital. I had developed an infection in my ankle which spread up my leg and into my groin area. It eventually turned into osteomyelitis, a bone infection from spending too much time in the ocean snorkeling. It eventually healed. I spent what was left of that summer surfing and messing around with Craig.

Surfing Accident, Dyslexia
9th Grade

The ninth grade was an exciting year because sports were a little more structured. The first semester was filled with flag football, which I played while some of the other kids played basketball. We played with other surrounding schools which I enjoyed. Competing with other schools created a real sense of camaraderie within the team.

I haven't talked much about the actual schoolwork itself because I wasn't very good at it. My teachers thought I had a reading disability called dyslexia. I didn't really understand because I thought I could read just fine. I just didn't perform well when it came to exams and tests. Mom decided to take me to different schools to test my reading skills. One was the Evelyn Wood School of Reading. It was determined that I was dyslexic with very low comprehension skills. My perplexed teachers would say, "He can read I can see his lips moving." The reading school I went to said I could read about three hundred words per minute with thirty percent comprehension. I knew I was a daydreamer and my mind would wander off. Still to this day, I'll be reading and find myself not knowing how I got to a particular page of a book and have to back up to where I could last remember I was and then start again. I later blamed it on my astrological sign, Pisces, who are supposedly daydreamers. The one positive thing the reading specialists discovered was that I had good dexterity skills. I was good at putting together puzzles.

That year we loaded up the B-26 Bomber and went back to Colorado Springs to show off our new little sister. Bill, Sandy and I stayed with our grandparents while Dave, Mom and new sister Patty stayed with Dave's father. Dave's mom had passed away some time ago. We didn't ski that trip because the snow wasn't very good so we all messed around with our non-skiing friends. Bill and all of his buddies were driving now so they were off doing car stuff. I can't remember what Sandy did. I hung around with my friend Morgan who didn't ski. We had spent a lot of time together growing up riding our bikes, swimming, hiking and exploring.

Morgan and some of his friends had planned to go to the Broadmoor Hotel and stage some prank. I didn't know what they were up to. I didn't have anything else to do so I joined them. We got into his friend's car and headed to the Broadmoor. I pretty much stayed out of the way. We went through the lobby and up the escalator to the lake across from the ice rink, which later became part of the Olympic-training center. Morgan's friends staged a shooting. They shot a dummy with a pistol loaded with blanks and threw the dummy in the lake. It was a big deal. I ran around to the other side of the lake by the ice skating arena. I never got caught and I don't think anyone else did either. The next day the newspaper headlines read "Killing at the Broadmoor". Since Dave had grown up at the Broadmoor it was of big interest to everyone in Colorado Springs. I didn't say anything for once. I was getting into enough trouble in those days. We flew back home a couple of days later and heard they had drained the lake and dredged the bottom but never found the dummy.

We had a wonderful Christmas with our new little sister Patty. She was curious about her surroundings and was making lots of new facial expressions. She was very interested in all the lights, shiny ornaments and tinsel. She was so much fun to watch and play with.

I was really looking forward to the spring semester at school with gymnastics and graduation ceremonies. It was going to be a fun time and a great way to bring junior high school to an end. In mid-January, just prior to the start of the spring semester, the surf was really good and big: the bigger the better. That's when I had my first surfing accident. I had just taken off on a good size wave when the wave started to close out; I slipped and straddled the board. I was in pain, but managed to get to shore. A friend's mom was on her way to pick her son up. He lived close to where I did and offered me a ride home. It seemed to take forever and we lived only 10 minutes away. I could feel swelling between my legs. Just as they pulled up in front of my house something broke open between my legs. I got out of the car grabbed my surfboard and held it behind me as I ran towards the house. I dropped my board, ran into the house and jumped up on the counter in the bathroom to look in the mirror, only to see blood everywhere. I grabbed a towel, put it between my legs and went into my parents' bedroom to tell them. Dave wanted to see, so I showed him and off to the hospital we went.

As it turned out, my doctor was the father of the girl who I had sat next to when I broke my arm in the sixth grade. They lived just down the street and I knew the whole family pretty well. He explained to me that the area between my legs that had broken open was of really no concern for a boy. However had it happened to a girl there would have been very different consequences because that area housed all the components necessary to have children. I remained in the hospital for a day or two. My case turned into a project for all the interns to see. A doctor came into the room with five or six interns to check out my injury. The doctor took his gloved fingers and slightly spread open my cheeks while I lay on my stomach. The blood squirted out all over their white coats. I laughed, but I don't think they were amused. The accident put an end to surfing for a while. Fortunately it didn't totally affect gymnastics for me, although the doctors advised not to do certain things.

Probably the most embarrassing part of this ordeal was that the only way to dress the wound was with a Kotex menstrual pad complete with a support strap. Needless to say, the word got out and everyone knew. It was also kind of funny because at the time, rather than taking a shop class, I was taking home economics. I got a lot of sympathy from the girls, which made a lot of guys jealous.

I was pretty much healed and had returned to all normal activities when, like an idiot, I rode a bike, jumped a curb and landed wrong straddling the bar. Well back to the hospital. This time they sewed me up. That was the first year since I was four that I hadn't gone skiing. I suppose between sports, injuries and girls there just wasn't enough time.

By the time summer arrived I was back to surfing, swimming and diving. When summer came to an end Mom was pregnant again and Bill was getting ready to go off to college. That's when Dave sat us all down for a serious discussion. We knew he wanted to talk to us, but had no idea what it was about. It turned out he wanted to adopt us. I supposed it was so we would all have the same last name of Maytag. We all loved Dave; the fact that he was our father was all that mattered to us. We weren't too concerned about the spelling of our last name, so we decided to remain Waltners. Bill went off to college and I prepared for high school.

High School Athletics, Mini
10th Grade

This year presented a new school, new friends and a new adventure for me. I always enjoyed the beginning of a new school year. It was great to see friends I hadn't seen all summer and meet new friends from different school districts. The athletic program in high school was the most sophisticated so far. I began football practice a month before school started. Because I was small I played 'B' football while the bigger kids played varsity. Bill had played football in high school and was quite good at it, which gave all the coaches high expectations from me. In some ways it was good, but I soon learned I didn't like playing second fiddle to anyone, especially my brother.

Since Bill had gone to Arizona to go to college and wouldn't be around much, I thought maybe he would be forgotten and I could get back to being me. I wasn't too worried. I had a lot of confidence when it came to sports. I played flanker. It was a fairly safe position, similar to that of a wide receiver, without all the blocking assignments. Being a football player was popular with the girls and I liked girls. I dated a cheerleader, who was probably the shortest girl in my class. Being the shortest boy we made a good couple.

Football was the last class, so it could carry over after school ended. My home economics class was right before football making for an easy afternoon. Life was good. We played our games early on Friday evening starting with junior varsity. The 'B' team went next, ending with the varsity game. The junior varsity squad was made up of kids too big to play 'B' football and not quite good enough to make the varsity squad. Practicing and playing football all week left the whole weekend open to surf, skateboard and catch up on any schoolwork I'd neglected during the week, which was a lot.

As football wound down and the holidays approached, time was spent with family and friends. Bill came home from college for Christmas and I was happy to see him. In college he had been given the nickname 'Willie' which has stuck to this day. I liked it, so it was easy for me to get used to. Not so for Mom and Dave. I never once heard them call him Willie.

While we were growing up in Colorado Springs, Bop had an old Crosley pickup truck that he let us drive on the farm. Willie and I couldn't wait to go to Moey and Bop's farm on Sundays for dinner and drive the Crosley. I got my learner's permit right after Willie left for college in the fall. Dave and I would drive quite a bit, but learning to drive on the freeways in Los Angeles was a lot different than driving on the farm.

In 1963, Dave bought one of the first Corvette Stingrays in California. It was black with red interior and had a 427 motor. It was very fast and turned heads everywhere he went. He let me drive it with him to play golf on the weekends. We got pulled over once because I looked so young. I didn't do anything wrong but the officer didn't even notice Dave in the passenger's seat. He let us go. Dave thought it was so funny, that he let me drive even more. Besides it was good practice for me.

When Willie was in high school Dave bought him a white Mini-Cooper with red interior that was going to be mine when I turned 16. I got to drive it prior to that up and down the drive like I had with the go-kart. I couldn't wait to turn 16. Dave loved his cars, airplanes and go-karts, anything with an engine. When Willie was still in high school Dave let him use the Stingray to go to the grocery store for Mom. On the way back home Willie rear-ended a car that had stopped to pick up a hitchhiker at the bottom of our road, the same place I used to hitchhike. When the police called Dave I thought he was going to kill Willie. I think the police officer thought so too. When Dave and I arrived at the scene of the accident the front of the Corvette was all over the road. Granted those cars were all fiberglass and it was definitely totaled. Dave got out of Mom's car and I stayed behind listening through the open window. After Dave surveyed the accident and saw that no one was hurt he looked at Willie and the cop and said "Well I guess it's time for a new one." That's how Willie got the Mini-Cooper. When he graduated from high school Dave bought him a Red Porsche that he let me drive while running errands for Mom and Dave. Dave was a pretty cool guy and so good to us!

The first semester came to an end. With a week off before starting the second semester Mom signed me up for a ski trip to June Mountain with the Santa Monica Ski Association. I met a lot of new kids from different high schools in Santa Monica. I immediately became a member and went to meetings once a month, and on two or three ski trips a year. I was really happy to be back on the ski scene again.

Second semester started in mid-January. Football was over so I took gymnastics which I really enjoyed. I knew I would from the taste I had gotten in junior high. I did all the disciplines, but excelled in long-horse vaulting and the high bar. Size didn't make any difference in gymnastics which was considered a varsity sport. My athletic career in high school was really shaping up. After my gymnastics workout, I would head down to the football field and watch a couple of my friends participate in their track and field workout. I was on a track and field team in Colorado Springs. The

50-yard dash, high jump and broad jump were my favorites.

Since I wasn't one to sit around, I decided to check out my track and field skills. Unlike football and gymnastics, track and field had a 'C' class. There were a lot of kids that tried out for track because they weren't rated by size, but ability. I was thinking there had to be something I could do out there that wouldn't interfere with gymnastics. Sure enough no one wanted to pole vault. Each class ('C' 'B' and varsity) only had a couple of athletes each. I gave it a try. I was good enough to make the 'C' team. There were only two of us who could vault over eight feet so I was in.

It was perfect. Gymnastic meets were on Fridays and track meets on Saturday mornings, leaving Saturday afternoons and Sundays for surfing, girls and skateboarding. My parents kept asking me, "When do you have time for your school work?" I didn't, but I didn't care. I just worked hard enough to get C's and C+'s and of course A's in gym class. I was popular with my classmates and coaches and what I lacked in the classroom I made up for in sports. I stayed very busy and didn't have time to get into much trouble, though I couldn't say that for all of my friends.

My 16th birthday finally arrived. Dave took me to my driving test. He made me do it in the Mini since it was my car, which was fine with me, but I didn't want the examiner to be uncomfortable in such a small vehicle. I barely passed the written part of the exam, which was to be expected because of my poor study habits, but I aced the driving part of it. It was a good feeling not to have to rely on anyone to cart me around anymore. Unfortunately, that feeling didn't last long because I got a speeding ticket two days later that I thought was unfair. I was on my way to school when an officer pulled me over. Being a new driver, I asked him what I was doing wrong? He answered me with a question. I hated that! "What's the speed limit?" I told him I didn't know. His comment was, "When you're driving a motor vehicle you should know the speed limit!" He told me I was traveling five miles over the speed limit. I thought that was a pretty cheap shot and he wrote me a ticket.

I was so scared to tell Dave. I knew I was going to lose my license. I did a little research even though it was no consolation, because everyone I talked to said,

I finally got a hand-me-down that fit. Girl not included! Bummer. Circa 1966

"Welcome to the club." Dave was mad and I was punished, and lost my license for two weeks, which felt like two years. It didn't take me long to realize that I was really punishing them. Now they had to drive Sandy and me around again so it probably felt like two years to them too. Patty was getting older, Mom was pregnant again and Dave was busy working to support his growing family. Once I got my license back I was the one who drove Sandy to her activities. We did a lot together anyway since we were only 22 months apart in age and she was only one year behind me in school. We were always close growing up.

After the first month of gymnastics and track, the swimming coach approached me and asked me about my diving skills. (One of my friends on the diving team had told him I could dive because he had seen me dive

Without athletics and girls, I wouldn't have gone to school.

at home in our pool.) I told him I used to dive in competitions when I was growing up in Colorado Springs. He told me there was a swim meet that afternoon and their diver was sick. He wanted to know if I could fill in. I told him he'd have to check with my gymnastics coach, and in the meantime I would go home and get my trunks. He said that he had already checked with my coach and he was okay with it. He also asked me what "trunks" were. I told him that they were what I wore to surf in. I asked him what kind of dives I would have to do and he told me I would need to do a front and back dive, an inward dive, a twisting dive and a reverse dive, otherwise known as a gainer. He asked me if I wanted to try and I said, "Sure." As I was driving home to get my trunks I wondered when the last time was that I had even attempted a reverse dive? I got my trunks and raced back to the pool which was only a couple of blocks from the school.

The swim meet had already started, but the diving portion of the meet was last. The coach told me I would have a little time to practice and get warmed up just before it was my turn. I decided to practice a reverse dive even though I had never done one. As I watched my competition I came to the realization that I would just have to wing the gainer. When it came time to choose my dives, I chose a double front flip in tuck position, a back flip in layout position, an inward flip in pike position and a front 1-1/2 flip with a full twist in free position (a position for twisting dives).

When it was time for the reverse dive I chose to do it in a tuck, which I knew would probably be a wild position, but all things considered I did pretty well. I won, but I didn't have much competition. Most all of my competitors' dives had a low degree of difficulty (front dives, back dives, not many inverted dives or flips).

I was promoted to varsity for the remaining meets that year, which meant all the points I received were tallied up with the varsity swim team. Coach Nelson, my swim coach, was so impressed with my diving skills that he wanted me to start training at Santa Monica City College with their school's diving coach. So after gymnastics and track I would go to SMCC to train three afternoons a week. The diving pool at SMCC was a really nice facility. Later that year I placed fourth in the city of Los Angeles Spring Board Diving meet. That same year I ended up lettering in football, track and field, gymnastics and diving, a school record, lettering in four different sports in one year.

Later that spring I went on one more ski trip with the Santa Monica Ski Association to June Mountain. I couldn't wait to go skiing. Just prior to going I saw my friend at a ski club meeting and asked if he was going also.

He said he was. I asked if he had a camera and he said he did. I told him to bring it. He asked why, so I opened the ski magazine and showed him a picture of Stein Eriksen upside down on skis in the air. He looked at me and said, "What are you crazy?" I said, "We'll see maybe." Sure enough, I did my first flip on skis and landed it perfectly. I probably did 10 more that day. I loved doing them.

Mom had a baby boy later that spring. He was named Dave for my stepfather. Our family was growing and everyone was very excited.

Sports, Surfing and Skiing
11th Grade

Football started a month before school and I still hadn't grown much. Mom and Dave were becoming more concerned. I didn't care much; I figured it would happen eventually. After all, my Mom was fairly tall over 5'7" and my Dad had been 6 feet. Before I knew it she had me seeing specialists who were x-raying my joints, knees, hips and shoulders. After several visits to the doctors they concluded that they found nothing abnormal and that I would eventually grow. They referred to me as a late bloomer. I wasn't too concerned. The only sport it may have made a difference in was football and I knew I wasn't going to pursue a professional football career. I was small, my car was small and my girlfriend was small… small was fine.

That year when Christmas came, Sandy and I went skiing with the ski club. We went the week before Christmas and Mom and Dave let me take the station wagon, the car that the nanny used. It was nice because I was able to take three other club members with me. We had a great trip and I helped several club members with their skiing.

We got home the day before Christmas with some good stories to share with Mom and Dave. I got another new surfboard for Christmas and spent the rest of the holiday break surfing with two of my other buddies that I skateboarded with as well. We were like the "Three Musketeers". We all had Mini-Coopers and surfed and skateboarded together. They were better than I was at both sports, but let me tag along anyway.

Spring semester was full of gymnastics, diving and track. I slowed down with track because my coaches wanted me to focus more on diving and long-horse vaulting. We had a big meet at Fairfax High School that spring which meant I would be competing on their three-meter high board. I had

Showing off as a newly elected vice-president of Santa Monica Ski Association.
Courtesy Dave Clement. June Lake, 1966

*My first big surfing contest,
Huntingdon Beach, California. Circa 1967*

been training quite a bit at SMCC on the three-meter board. I wanted to show my coach a new dive I was working on, a 2-1/2 front somersault in pike position. It was a beautiful dive and I nailed it. Unfortunately, I hit the bottom of the pool pretty hard. When I came to the surface a bunch of competitors were at the side of the pool looking at me. I thought they were there to tell me what a great dive it was, but as I was getting out of the pool I looked at the water and there was blood everywhere. I had split my head open and they were there to help me out of the pool. Off to the hospital I went to get sewed up. At this point I lost count of all the stitches I had received and I was still just in high school.

I skied quite a bit that winter. I skied locally whenever I could. That year during the long school break, I went on three or four trips with the ski club. I also continued with diving training and felt confident by the time I competed in the LA meet. I competed against a kid from Beverly Hills High School. We were respectful rivals, but good friends considering we hardly ever saw each other, only two or three times a year competing at meets. In our final meet, he finished second and I came in fourth. As we were warming up for this particular meet I noticed I was having some trouble on the three-meter board. I kept slipping on my approach. It scared me and I asked my friend about it, as it was his "home" pool. He agreed and said that all the divers had been complaining about it all year. Well it scared me so much I changed all of my dives except for my back dive and my inward dive because they didn't require an approach. I moved to the low board which meant my degree of difficulty would not be as high overall because three of my dives were done on the one-meter board. That left only two on the three-meter high board. I ended up in fifth place and my friend won the meet. I was really happy for him and totally OKAY with my finish and that I didn't require any more stitches. Whew! I did get a second place finish in the Western Division Diving Championship that year and lettered in three disciplines: football, gymnastics and diving.

I also surfed in my first contest that summer at Huntington Beach, doing pretty well. I loved competition even though I didn't win. I really enjoyed the excitement and the atmosphere.

The first national skateboard championship was held downtown in the LA coliseum. I wasn't good enough to compete, but two of my surfing buddies placed first and second. That was huge as the competitors came from all over the world. They were cast in a "Tony the Tiger" cereal commercial ("They're Great!"). We all thought skateboarding was pretty funny. Later that year, John, my friend who had won first place, appeared on the television show "What's My Line?" where the question was asked, "Would the *real skateboarder* please stand up?" I don't think he lived that down until he graduated from high school.

Graduation, Porsche
12th Grade

A month prior to school starting, as football practice got underway, I was skateboarding with John and stubbed my toe. We were both on the same skateboard going way too fast and he jumped off. I'm lucky all I did was stub my toe (the one next to the big toe), but it ended up getting infected and got so bad I had to have surgery. The doctor had to remove about a quarter inch of the bone. He tucked the loose skin back into the end of the toe and stitched it together with "wire" stitches, a novelty for me. The doctor kept a close eye on it because I was very prone to infections.

When the stitches were removed, I asked the doctor if my toe was always going to look a little deformed. He told me if I wanted

My sister Sandy and me posing for Volkswagen. Santa Monica. 1967

I could get a fake nail and glue it on the toe, because the natural nail was never going to grow back. I didn't care what it looked like, but I was worried about wearing ski boots. He told me it would be fine, as long as I kept it clean, stayed out of the ocean and wore a shoe big enough not to interfere with the healing process.

So that year I decided not to play football, surf or skateboard and just take it easy, which was the hard part. After being hit from behind in the Mini that summer (which broke my heart I loved that car) Dave bought me a Buick Opel. After all Sandy was still six months away from getting her driver's license, and Mom and Dave needed another driver in the family.

I was excused from all athletic activities in school, so I played with my new car, worked out in the weight room at school and helped out with the football team during practice and at the games, so I could still feel like part of the team. I was also very active in the ski club and was elected vice president of the Santa Monica Ski Association that fall. It consumed a lot of my time, but I was excited for the challenge.

Earlier in junior high I was president of the student council and vice president of the ninth grade class. I was able to use some of those experiences to help me with the duties of my new ski club position. Handling all the fundraising activities I organized and put together three ski trips for the upcoming '67-'68 ski season. I planned a trip the week before Christmas, one in mid-January and one in March. My toe had healed by early November and I was able to put my ski boots on, which was a relief.

My toe never did return to its original size. It was always a little bit bigger, so I had to be careful with the type of shoe I wore. Ski boots in those days were a lot like hiking boots are today. The only noticeable difference was that ski boots had buckles. Of course our skis were a lot longer and so were our poles.

The holidays came and our first ski trip was a big success. We had more

A couple of flips for the crowd. Courtesy John Hunt. June Lake, California. Circa 1966.

people than ever before and we had to hire a bus service to handle all our skiers. I spent a lot of time organizing the on snow activities once we arrived at June Lake. I also found myself helping many of the new skiers get a feel for skiing. I really enjoyed helping the weaker skiers. This sport has been so good to me. It is always a pleasure sharing my skills with others. I still did my flips and organized a fun race for all those who wanted to participate. We had a lot of fun. It was always a good trip when everyone returned in one piece.

Christmas was great. I loved watching my little brother and sister open their gifts and play with their toys. When Sandy and I got home from the ski trip we took one look at the tree and could barely see it, hidden in all the wrapped gifts. Extremely generous, Dave loved Christmas and the spirit of giving. The day after Christmas was exciting too. It was Sandy's birthday and yes, Dave gave her a Pontiac Firebird complete with ribbon and bow. Sandy was so excited and I was too mostly because I didn't have to chauffeur her around anymore!

As the New Year got underway I was looking forward to my last semester of high school.

Unfortunately the whole world was concerned about the Vietnam War. By 1968 we were in the thick of it. You couldn't go anywhere or read anything without the war being the main topic. We were all scared, mostly because of the uncertainty of the whole situation. At school, after school and on the weekends, the war was all anyone talked about. It was a scary time for all.

Diving was the only sport I competed in during my entire senior year. I was injured during football season and had lost interest in track. My gymnastics coach wanted me to decide between gymnastics and skiing. I wasn't going to stop skiing, but I understood his position. He felt as though I had a chance for a college scholarship if I trained hard and didn't get hurt. At this point deep inside, I knew I wanted to pursue a career in skiing. I wasn't sure what it was, but I knew I loved the mountains, the snow and everything about that kind of life. I loved the ocean, but if I had to pick between the two, I would choose the mountains.

A friend of mine who I skied with in the Santa Monica Ski Association went to Alta and worked on the ski patrol and bussing tables at the High Rustler Lodge. We stayed in contact and he invited me to come and compete in the National Gelandesprung Championships. I showed up and earned my room and board by performing a flip every afternoon over an outside bar carved in the snow. When I first got there everyone was curious where I had come from. I was out jumping the hill in the practice rounds which meant traveling 130 to 140 feet in the air, but everyone got to know me from flipping over the bar at the High Rustler Lodge.

Later that spring I competed in the Gelandesprung event. A huge jump had been built on a mine dump at the bottom of the ski area. It was a big air contest on skis and very intimidating. All the big names in the ski business competed there. People came from all over the world: ski school directors, ski racers, ex-ski racers, ski instructors and the list went on. Alta was known for having the best powder skiing in the world. With the event happening annually in the spring, it was basically a big end of the season party.

I ended up in fourth place in the competition, just out of the money. I didn't get hurt and thought that was an accomplishment by itself because there were some unbelievable crashes. I got to know a lot of people in the ski industry and was welcomed back the next year. While flying home from Utah to graduate from high school, I reminisced about the whole trip. That's when I knew that I wanted to pursue a career as a ski professional.

I graduated from high school and was given a Porsche for a graduation

First road trip in my new Porsche. 1968

present. It was SO COOL, I loved it. There were only a few 911s in California at the time. With the Vietnam War at its peak and the draft in full gear, I spent the summer trying to figure out how to keep from being drafted. We all were. I decided to talk to an attorney who specialized in keeping people out of the war. He felt it would be easy for me because of all my medical issues. At 5'3", I was borderline to the height requirement to be drafted. I also had back problems from all the impact sports I had done while in high school.

All I needed now was $2000 so I ran it by Dave. He was extremely disappointed in me. He wanted me to go to college or take a chance on getting drafted and serve my country proudly. He felt I would be missing out on a great opportunity for an education. So I attended Santa Monica City College. I was never very good in school and college was so crowded from everyone avoiding the draft that I felt like the experience was just an extension of high school with ashtrays.

After three months in college I decided to take a chance on the draft. I had letters from my doctors that I had never given to the attorney. With mixed emotions rolling around in my head I packed my Porsche, moved to June Lake to pursue my long awaited skiing career and seek a job as a ski instructor.

Off to June Lake
November 1968

I had never moved away from home and Dave wasn't very happy with me. I still wasn't entirely convinced I was doing the right thing and was uncertain about what was ahead of me. I didn't want to go to war, but I didn't want to go to college either. Not having a job or a place to live, I felt as though I was taking a huge risk.

As I was leaving home I was thinking there was no turning back now. It's about a five-hour drive to June Lake and fortunately I had my friend Greg to help me find a job and a place to live. He said I could stay with him. He was the only person there who even knew I was coming. I had met the ski school director before and had mentioned to him jokingly that if things didn't work out in college I might see him next fall, but that was eight months ago. I arrived late that afternoon, glad the drive was over. I went through every scenario you could imagine and was thoroughly worn out. I thought I would be really excited, but I wasn't. After I unpacked the car and went to bed my last thought was if worse came to worse I'd just go back home with my tail between my legs.

The next morning was absolutely beautiful, snowcapped peaks and bright blue sky. Greg worked on the ski patrol and kept assuring me that things would be fine, so I got my ski clothes on, grabbed my skis and boots and off we went. My mom had given me some money to help me get started. She was actually the only one who supported my decision, most likely because being a ski instructor herself; she knew what I was up against. She told me not to tell Dave that she had given me the money, so I didn't.

The front of June Mountain was very steep and designed differently from most ski areas. A chairlift took you to mid-mountain where everything was located: the restaurant, ski patrol, ski rentals and the ski school. I walked into the restaurant with Greg and was totally surprised at how welcomed I was by everyone. As it turned out, Greg had told everyone I was coming. Bill Sim, the ski school director, came up shook my hand and welcomed me. He told me that after he took care of the morning classes we could talk. I was feeling so much better by then.

I walked out with him and watched as he assigned the lessons. It was pretty slow being the middle of the week and several weeks before the Christmas holidays. We went out and skied. He told me that he wasn't sure if he could use me and that I might need some training. For the next couple of weeks I trained with the school and he was pleased with my progress. He told me he didn't need me the week before Christmas, but to show up the day after Christmas. I found a place to live and went back home for Christmas to get some more things. I returned to June Lake on Christmas day. Mom gave me enough money for my first month's rent and Dave was actually feeling better about my decision.

Now I was excited. I showed up the day after Christmas like Bill had told me to do. I didn't get a lesson that day, but a couple of days later the ski school ran out of instructors and needed someone for a private lesson. Bill looked at me and said, "Here's your chance" with a big smile on his face. When the lesson with a mom and daughter from LA ended they seemed happy and so was I. At the end of the day Bill came up to me and told me they really enjoyed their lesson. He offered me a job. I immediately called Mom and Dave to tell them the news. They were very happy for me and I think a little relieved. I had a job and a place to live. Life was good for the spoiled little rich kid from southern California.

Now all I had to worry about was being drafted. I had already received one notice to report for my pre-induction physical. My attorney told me I could receive two notices, but when I got the third one I needed to report. After that if I didn't report, I'd go directly to boot camp and take my physical there. I had read in the newspaper that the government was going to schedule the first ever lottery for the draft sometime that spring and it was going to be televised.

I worked through the Christmas holidays and was really enjoying my new life. When January came, things were pretty slow during the week, but quite busy on the weekends. Bill kept us busy with on-snow training. I spent one night a week at his house with others who wanted to attend a study group. We studied a teaching manual prepared by the Professional Ski Instructors of America (PSIA) for ski instructors who wanted to prepare themselves for the certification exam, which was being held in Squaw Valley on the north shore of Lake Tahoe that spring. Bill's house was just up the road from where I was renting my cabin. I spent a lot of time with him. He sort of put me under his wing and was a mentor to me. Bill was very well respected in the PSIA. He represented the United States in 1968 in Aspen, Colorado at the eighth Interski event. It was a competition where ski schools from around the world would come together to compete and demonstrate the different techniques used in skiing and ski teaching.

One evening in late January, I left Bill's house on a beautiful, starlit night around 10:00 p.m. I went to bed in my little cabin. The next morning, as I was leaving to go to work, I couldn't get out the front door. It had snowed six feet overnight and it was still snowing a foot an hour. The Sierras are known for lots of snow, but I had never seen anything like this. I dug myself out and literally climbed through the snow to Bill's house. When Bill saw me with that big grin on his face he said, "Welcome to the Sierras." We dug his house and his car out, but even with four-wheel drive and chains on all four wheels we weren't going anywhere until the roads were plowed.

Bill's house and my cabin were west of the ski area and the town of June Lake was east of it. We knew it would be awhile before the plows would get to us. It was around noon and it had snowed three to four more feet since I had left my cabin earlier that morning. "Quiet," Bill said. You could barely hear the sound of large snowplows. They weren't that close. Out there in the middle of nowhere you could hear a pin drop a half-mile away. Within an hour a large Austin-Western road grader was in front of the house. Harley was the driver's name and also the local sheriff. Bill and I got in the grader next to Harley. As he plowed the road there was no telling where the side of the road was. All of a sudden it dawned on me that my Porsche was out there somewhere and I didn't want Harley to hit it. He managed to plow around it

Sierra cement and a ton of it. Courtesy of John Hunt.

and Harley gave me a couple of long poles that the highway department used to mark the roads to place around my car so no one would hit it.

The ski area was closed until further notice. No one was going anywhere. The grocery store was almost out of everything; milk, produce and even canned goods were limited. It finally stopped snowing and things slowly got back to normal. We had to dig out the ski area and shoveling snow was the only work to be had. I didn't go to college, but I had definitely earned my PhD in shoveling (pile higher and deeper).

Rumor had it that a 75-foot crane had been lost at Mammoth ski area when the storm came in, but they decided to leave it until spring. They knew where it was because they had used it the summer before installing the gondola which accessed the bottom of the ski area to the top of what was called "The Cornice".

When June Mountain finally reopened, we rode the chairlift that accessed the top of the mountain. For the last 300 yards our skis were actually on the snow. When we got off the lift we climbed up and out of the unloading area to ski down the mountain. IT WAS WILD! It took a while for things to return to normal as far as the ski business went. It was extremely difficult for anyone wanting to ski to get from LA to the ski areas in the Sierras.

We shoveled roofs and driveways anything that needed snow removal to pay our bills while waiting for the skiing public to arrive from the city. There wasn't much work teaching, so I took the opportunity to train, not only on snow, but also with Bill in the evenings to better prepare myself for the

Oops! Too late now. Fill your Sitzmark! Courtesy of John Hunt. 1969

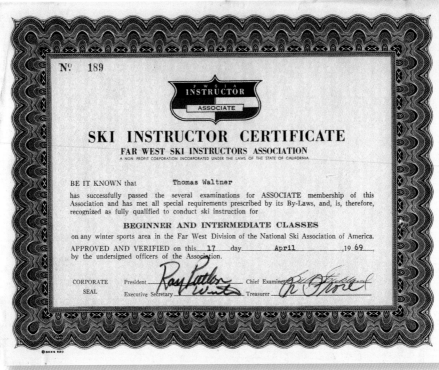

Nº 189

SKI INSTRUCTOR CERTIFICATE

FAR WEST SKI INSTRUCTORS ASSOCIATION

A NON PROFIT CORPORATION INCORPORATED UNDER THE LAWS OF THE STATE OF CALIFORNIA

BE IT KNOWN that   Thomas Waltner

has successfully passed the several examinations for ASSOCIATE membership of this Association and has met all special requirements prescribed by its By-Laws, and, is, therefore, recognized as fully qualified to conduct ski instruction for

BEGINNER AND INTERMEDIATE CLASSES

on any winter sports area in the Far West Division of the National Ski Association of America.

APPROVED AND VERIFIED on this **17** day **April** ,19 **69** by the undersigned officers of the Association.

CORPORATE SEAL

President _____ Chief Examiner _____

Executive Secretary _____ Treasurer _____

The first time I can honestly say I passed a test without cheating. 1969

One proud ski instructor. 1969.

certification exams in the spring. I was learning that there was a lot more to becoming a good ski instructor than just being a good skier.

Finally the grocery store started to fill back up with food, which was a sign that the main road between June Mountain and LA was clearing up. We became a ski area again and went back to work. I was able to get my car dug out. Fortunately, it wasn't hit by any snowplows during this ordeal. We heard stories of cars that lined the road from the town of Mammoth up to the ski area that had either been wrecked by the snowplows or, in some cases, abandoned by tourists who just wanted to get out and return to their homes in LA.

I moved from my cabin into town and lived with a couple of Germans I worked with, Heinz and Herman. Heinz also had a Porsche he brought from Germany when he moved to the U.S. I received my second notice to report for my pre-induction physical, for which I didn't report. I knew I could wait until the third notice before I had to go.

As spring approached, several of us loaded up in a couple of cars and headed to Squaw Valley for the certification exam. We were all well prepared because of the time we spent studying due to the snowy winter. I was looking forward to skiing Squaw Valley. I had been to the Tahoe area once before and skied Heavenly Valley and Alpine Springs just north and west of Squaw Valley.

The exam was all on snow, yet broken up into two categories; free skiing skills and other technical skills, which included demonstration of learning skills and the teaching methodology. The skiing skills were my strongest part of the exam. I did well on the demos, but probably the most difficult of them was the slow speed you had to use when demonstrating them. So much of learning is done by visual interpretation of the movements necessary to achieve what you are learning. The verbal explanation of teaching skills was the most difficult for me. I had to rely totally on my athletic ability. When the results were posted I was extremely nervous reading the list of names of those who passed. I made the list! I passed! I thought I did well in both skiing and the on snow demonstrations, but the actual teaching I just didn't know.

I saw Bill immediately following the results. He had that big grin that he wore on his face when he was happy. He was proud of me and later told me that the examiners wanted to grant me full certification status, but couldn't because of my experience and age.

We arrived back in June Lake right before our Spring Carnival. It was my first carnival and I didn't know what to expect. There was a parade in town with several in-town activities. There was beer slalom in the afternoon and a torchlight parade down the front of the mountain that evening. I represented the ski school in the beer slalom, which consisted of eight gates with a Colt 45 beer at each gate, which the racer had to consume before going to the next gate. Not being a boozer and still too young to drink, I got drunk even though I threw up at each gate. I had consumed enough to get hammered.

I was supposed to lead the torchlight parade that night, but everyone felt I was too drunk to participate, so they sent me down on the lift. As the skiers in the torchlight parade skied under the lift rather than turning over my shoulder to watch, I chose to watch between my legs. Drunk as I was, I rolled out of the chair forward fell 25 feet and landed on my back in the pike position in about eight feet of snow. I was stuck. My feet and hands were straight up in the air and I was unable to breathe easily. People were running up to see if I was OKAY and all I heard was Harley the sheriff saying, "Don't move him he may be paralyzed." I barely had enough air to say, "Get me out of here!" Greg was there and helped me out. I thought it was pretty funny, but no one else did. In hindsight I was lucky either because I was drunk, or because of all the snow, or perhaps both. That hole in the snow was there for the rest of the year. Because I had been given a nickname earlier that season of "Spoony" (people thought I was born with a silver spoon in my mouth) the hole was referred to as "Spoony's Landing."

Ski season ended and I received my third draft notice and this time I had to report for my pre-induction physical in downtown LA. I picked up my last paycheck, packed my car and headed back home to LA for the thing that scared me the most, being drafted. I showed up at the downtown draft headquarters at 5:00 a.m. with all the letters I had from doctors I had seen in high school. I was scared and didn't know what to expect. I got in line and followed until I was told what to do next.

There were a lot of different stations where your weight, height, eyes and ears were checked. I just followed a green line on the floor from station to station, until I got to a station where I went into a private room, sat down and talked to an army doctor. At this station the examiner wanted to see all the letters I had from my doctors. As he scrutinized the letters he glanced up at me and said, "What do you do, these letters indicate your health isn't very good and maybe you should be confined to a bed?" I told him I was a teacher, a ski instructor. He thought I was kidding. Now I was back peddling and not being a very good liar. I told him I only taught beginners as it only required a little strength and it was about the only exercise I could do. Thankfully, he had never skied. He kept my letters and I continued down the green line.

When I got to the next station, they took about 30 of us at a time and we all stood in a circle. I had heard about this station. This is where they had you take your clothes off, bend over and cough. We all stood there stark naked as the officer walked around the circle from the inside. When he got to me he stopped, looked down at my feet and asked, "Do they hurt?" I replied, "My feet?"

"Yes your feet!" I looked at him and said, "Not really." I looked down and saw that he was referring to my toe. It had been cramped up in ski boots all winter and was swollen and red. I was hoping this was a good thing.

I put my clothes back on and went to the next station. I waited there for a while and when it was my turn I walked up to the desk. The man there looked at me; stamped the paper I carried to each station and told me to follow the green line until I got to the red line, then follow the red line. The red line took me back to where I had started. I looked at the paper he had stamped and it said in bold black letters, "REJECTED." This was truly the happiest day of my life. All 19 years of it.

I drove home and immediately made several phone calls. I had made a lot of friends in June Lake and they were all concerned about the draft. They knew I wasn't a good candidate for the army. The next couple of days were spent looking for a job, surfing and catching up with some high school buddies. I started working as a cashier at the same beach club where I learned to play beach volleyball with my neighbors Ed and Bob. That lasted a few weeks until I was offered a job teaching swimming. I enjoyed teaching little kids to swim. It was a lot of work, with a lot of responsibility.

Two of my friends I had gone to high school with, Mark and Rick were going to Europe. Rick ordered a Volkswagen bus and was going to pick it up at the factory in Germany. It sounded like it was going to be a great trip traveling around Europe in a Volkswagen bus. I went to the airport with them to say goodbye and told them if I could, I would meet them in Germany when they picked up the bus. Driving home from the airport I started thinking. If I sold my Porsche, went to Germany and bought another Porsche, an older model similar to the one Heinz had in June Lake, I could ship it back to the U.S. It would pay for the trip and I could travel around Europe with Mark and Rick and come home to a different Porsche, "Cool." After all, I had three weeks to put it all together, "HA! Good luck!"

3 M's Surf Spot. Ensenada, Mexico. Circa 1969.

First I called Heinz to ask him if he knew someone in Germany who could help me buy a car. He told me he had a friend in Hamburg who had a Porsche dealership. I called to check on a charter flight to Europe, the same company Rick and Mark had used. There was a flight going to Stockholm, Sweden, which would work if I could be ready to leave in ten days. Now all I had to do was sell my car. I didn't have much time if I was going to pull this off.

When I got up the next morning, my mom asked me if I was late for work. I told her I had quit my job and was going to Europe to meet Mark and Rick. She looked at me in shock and told me there was no way I could do that! I replied, "Watch me! If I couldn't make it work I wouldn't go." Mom told me not to ask her for anything. She didn't think I had a chance in hell to pull it off.

I sold my car and jumped on the plane to Stockholm and stayed there for a couple of days. I'll never forget how beautiful the Tivoli Gardens were. I jumped a train from Sweden to Hamburg and contacted Heinz's friend as soon as I got there. He had just received the letter from Heinz telling him I was coming. He picked me up at my hotel and took me to his dealership where I promptly bought a car. It took a couple of days to arrange to have it shipped back home and to finalize the transaction.

On Friday he drove me to the edge of town and made me a sign so I could hitchhike to Wiedenbruck, Germany, a small farming community where the Volkswagen bus factory was located. The only way to get there was by car. A family who lived in the small town picked me up. We drove late into the night and they dropped me off at a small motel where we said our good-byes.

The next morning, the motel owner took me to the factory where I planned to meet up with Mark and Rick on Monday morning. Being the weekend, the factory was closed and there was no way to find them until then. I felt I had gotten a lot accomplished in the last week, especially not speaking any of the languages I encountered. Everyone I met was really helpful. I'm sure they thought it was a little strange seeing a kid traveling by himself buying a car and hoping to meet up with a couple of friends who had no idea he was even in Europe, let alone in the town where they were to hook up. Needless to say, I prayed all weekend long that things would work out.

On Monday morning the motel owner drove me to the factory at 8:00 a.m. when it opened. I walked in the building and asked the receptionist if Mark and Rick were there? She told me they were upstairs in the observation lounge over-looking the assembly area, having coffee and rolls while they

Hussongs Cantina. Ensenada Mexico. Circa 1969.

waited to take delivery of their bus. She escorted me to where they were. As they came into sight, I called out, "Morning guys I'm here." As they turned and saw me, the look on their faces was priceless. I asked them if they ever

thought I would actually make it. Their response was they never gave it another thought. I replied "Let the ride begin!" Brand new car, good friends, and off to Amsterdam to pick up the surfboards they sent before leaving for Europe. Amsterdam was the first stop of a one-month tour of camping and exploring Europe.

Hitchhiking from Hamburg to Wiedenbruck, Germany

Tivoli Gardens. Stockholm, Sweden

Porsche Dealership. Hamburg, Germany. 1969

Let this safari begin

40

Mark and I left Rick in Biarritz, France and we rode the train to Paris, the Hovercraft to London, and flew back to the states. Rick ended his trip in Morocco, where he had the bus shipped back to the U.S.; arriving back home about three weeks after Mark and I returned. It was a great reunion. We watched the lunar landing at Rick's house, talked about our trip and what was next.

Twenty years later while visiting Mark, I learned that Rick had paid his way through college, had become an engineer, worked for an oil company, bought a small Cessna airplane, moved to Santa Barbara, got married and lived in a beautiful upscale neighborhood. I asked Mark where he had gotten the money to do everything. He proceeded to tell me that when Rick was in Morocco he filled his bus with Moroccan hash, shipped it back to the U.S., and sold it all. I looked at Mark and said, "Rick never even smoked the stuff!" Mark told me that Rick had planned this long before we even went to Europe and it was his secret.

I packed my new Porsche and headed back to work at June Lake with some great memories of that summer. I couldn't wait to show Heinz my new car. After all he was the one who made it all happen: the trip, the car and all the great memories.

But why would you want to? Girls! *Biarritz, France. 1969.*

42

SEVENTIES

Dogs, Dirt, and Dope
Winter 1969-1970

I arrived in June Lake and rented a trailer in town above the Heidelberg Lodge, a place I was familiar with from my trips with the Santa Monica Ski Club. My friend Greg lived with me that winter. Greg had acquired a nickname at the end of the previous year which seemed to stick because everyone now referred to him as "Wolfy." It was a very appropriate name because he had a wolf man-like hairline in the front of his head. I saw Heinz briefly when I arrived. He and Herman both had gotten jobs in Sun Valley and were going there to teach for the winter. Bill also took a job as ski school director at Boreal Ridge, a ski area in the Tahoe area close to Truckee, California. It seemed as if June Lake was a stepping-stone for professionals to get experience before moving to bigger areas.

That winter we had a new ski school director, an Austrian named Bruno Binder. I liked Bruno and having Stage I Certification, along with one year of experience at June Mountain, I was able to get as much work as I wanted. After the holidays were over and things slowed down, Bruno came to me and said, "People tell me you can do flips on skis." I told him I could, but hadn't for a year. He asked if I was willing to do a show every day at 1:00 p.m. in front of the guests at the restaurant just prior to the afternoon lessons to try and drum up a little business. I agreed to do it. I liked doing them and it seemed to work. A film crew from LA came up to film me for a ski show which aired on T.V. every Sunday evening in LA. I never did see it, but I heard all about it.

The Hart ski rep came to June Lake to demo skis and to check on one of his accounts in town. He skied with Bruno and demoed skis to all the instructors. He saw my show and asked if I would flip on Hart skis and Rosemont boots. Of course I said yes; I had never been offered free equipment before.

I spent all winter preparing for the Stage II Certification exam and was excited to take my career to the next level. I was also excited because it was at Mammoth that spring. I had skied Mammoth a lot and was familiar with the mountain. It was more difficult that year than the previous year at Squaw. There was a written exam and an on-snow question and answer session. I felt pretty good about the written portion so it was just a matter of getting through the on-snow part. They asked me why I wanted to be a ski instructor and totally caught me off guard. My answer was pretty simple.

I told them, "I really enjoy teaching people to do something that I have enjoyed doing my whole life."

I personally didn't think that was the answer they wanted to hear. They discussed and evaluated my "on-snow" portion of the exam right in front of me. The head examiner looked right at me and said, "Congratulations. You are now a fully certified ski instructor." I was very excited because it was not only a relief, but also a great way to end the season.

Not knowing what I was going to do that upcoming summer, I packed my stuff and went back home, only to find out that Mom and Dave were getting a divorce. They wanted to tell me in person and asked Sandy not to say anything when she came up earlier to ski that Spring. Mom wanted to move back to Colorado and decided to move to Denver. She had some friends there and it was close to Colorado Springs. I helped her move with Patty and David, which took the better part of the summer.

She asked me what my plans were for the upcoming ski season. I told her I was going to return to June Lake and teach there. She suggested I try to find a job in Colorado. She wanted me to be close to her and felt I would be better off being a "small fish in a big sea as opposed to a big fish in a small pond." I laughed and thought back to Bill and Heinz moving on to bigger ski areas.

In 1969 there were only a handful of major ski resorts in Colorado. They were: Winter Park, Breckenridge, Steamboat Springs, Vail and Aspen. I called and made appointments with all of the ski school directors in those areas. Jim Hammock, a friend I knew from California, was working for Shell Oil based in Houston, Texas. He was in Denver at an oil convention. When the convention ended we loaded up his rental car and made a loop through the different ski areas with Aspen being the last stop before returning to Denver.

When we pulled into Aspen I looked over at him and said, "Well that was a waste of time. This is where I want to be." All the memories I had of Aspen growing up, learning to ski there in the mid-fifties, really hit home for me. We pulled into a small hotel on Main Street, the Cortina Lodge, next to Carl's Pharmacy. My appointment with the ski school director was at 2:00 p.m. that afternoon, so we got settled in the hotel and walked over to Carl's Pharmacy. They had a soda fountain style lunch counter and we sat down and ordered a cheeseburger and a milkshake. Directly behind us was a magazine rack with a Time Magazine, which had a cover story featuring Aspen. I grabbed it and opened it up to the cover story. In bold letters it read, "Aspen" with the subtitle, "Dogs, Dirt and Dope." I felt right at home. I had a dog, there were only two paved streets (Main and Galena) and I had been known to smoke a little dope.

I met with Curt Chase, the director of the ski school. He didn't hire me, telling me that everyone who came to Aspen to teach skiing had to take a hiring clinic, so Jim and I returned to Denver. Feeling pretty confident and being fully certified, I packed up my Porsche, my dog Amos and headed to Aspen.

Upside down with my new skis. Courtesy John Hunt. Circa 1970

Sporting my new boots and skis. Courtesy John Hunt. Circa 1970

Nº 268

FWSIA
INSTRUCTOR
CERTIFIED

SKI INSTRUCTOR CERTIFICATE
FAR WEST SKI INSTRUCTORS ASSOCIATION
A NON PROFIT CORPORATION INCORPORATED UNDER THE LAWS OF THE STATE OF CALIFORNIA

BE IT KNOWN that   THOMAS WALTNER

has successfully passed the several examinations for CERTIFIED membership of this Association and has met all special requirements prescribed by its By-Laws, and, is, therefore, recognized as fully qualified to conduct ski instruction for

ALL CLASSES

on any winter sports area in the Far West Division of the National Ski Association of America.
APPROVED AND VERIFIED on this 3rd day MAY 19 70 by the undersigned officers of the Association.

CORPORATE   President   Chief Examiner
SEAL   Executive Secretary   Treasurer

The second time I can honestly say I passed a test without cheating. 1970

Me and Mom. June Lake, CA. Circa 1969

48

Wild Bird, Gun and Hashish
Winter 1970-1971

I didn't have a place to live when I arrived in Aspen, but Mom had given me a little money to help me get started. After all, she was the one who wanted me to be a small fish in a big sea. When we were there in the early fall, I had met Jim's friends Don and Jeanie Lemos. Peter Greene, who had dated my mom and taught me to ski in the early fifties, also lived there with his wife Mary Anne. I'll never forget as a seven year old in Colorado Springs, Peter proposing to my mom and her feeling he wasn't the right guy for her at the time.

The first night in town I stayed at the Cortina Lodge and just by luck I ran into my friend Jamie, who I had gone to high school with. He graduated a year ahead of me and had moved to Aspen about a year ago. Jamie had a place to live on the edge of town and offered me his couch until I could find a place of my own.

In pursuit of my own place to live, I visited with Don and Jeanie several times and spent time with Peter and Mary Anne. I helped Peter with some small projects around his house, which was a good way to keep me busy while looking for a place to live and waiting to go to work. Later, one of Jamie's roommates moved to Denver to pursue a career in journalism, so I was able to move into his room. The timing couldn't have been better with winter approaching and me without a place to live.

Prior to the lifts opening, Don took me up Independence Pass to hike and ski the Fourth of July Bowl at the top of the Pass. I was surprised to see how many local people skied up there. The views were absolutely beautiful and I felt like I was on top of the world. Two days before opening day, I was sitting outside having breakfast at the Epicurious Restaurant with a couple of my new friends. They weren't too concerned about the lack of snow even though it hadn't snowed since early November. They kept saying, "It will come." Sure enough, the next day it started dumping. It reminded me of June Mountain, the only difference being it snowed two or three inches an hour in the Rockies, where in the Sierras it was measured in feet per hour. It made for a beautiful Thanksgiving Day opening.

The hiring clinic started the following Monday morning. I showed up at the bottom of Aspen Mountain, or "Ajax" as referred to by the locals, for ski school orientation. We were divided into different groups. Returning instructors went off with their respective clinic leaders and the new people were divided up into two groups. Those with teaching experience were in one group and those with none were in the other. The group I was in, those of us with teaching experience, got on the lift, went to the top of the mountain and into the Sundeck Restaurant. It took three lifts and 45 minutes to get to the top. Once inside we had coffee, warmed up and introduced ourselves explaining where we had previously taught, along with our level of certification or experience. Not only was I nervous not knowing what to expect, but I was impressed by the level of professionalism involved. Once we got our skis on I settled down a little and not lacking in my skiing abilities began to feel more comfortable.

Every school had a different approach to teaching and in this case it wasn't any different. I'm thankful to have had Bill back in June Lake as my first ski school director. He was always up-to-date on teaching techniques, a great teacher and technician, who took special attention when training me. I now greatly appreciated that. The hiring clinic was a week-long clinic. We were evaluated on free skiing demonstrations, teaching skills and communication skills. It was a tough week, educationally enlightening and very valuable to my career.

I was hired and assigned to the Snowmass ski school. I was expecting to get hired, but we were given a choice of which mountain we wanted to teach on. Working on Ajax was out of the question as someone had to die or need to be replaced in order to be assigned to Ajax. I wanted to teach at Buttermilk so I made an appointment to see Curt Chase, the ski school director, to find out why I was assigned to Snowmass. Curt told me that I did well in the hiring clinic and my skills and experience were more valuable to him if I went to Snowmass, which made me feel good. I thanked him for hiring me and told him I would do the best job I could. I was well received at Snowmass and made a lot of new friends. The head supervisor at Snowmass, Horst Abrams, and I got along great. He helped me a lot with my teaching and skiing skills.

Mom came up several times that winter and we experienced a lot of Aspen together. She knew it well because of the past, although it had changed quite a bit. Even though I came as a young kid; now as an adult, I could appreciate all it had to offer. We went to the Crystal Palace several times for the dinner show, the Aspen Inn to see the Nitty Gritty Dirt Band, and of course all the other local favorites.

At our end of the season party I did several flips and raced Stein Eriksen in his annual race against the ski instructors. Stein had been the ski school supervisor the previous year, but now worked as the director of skiing at

Deer Valley. He came back each year to host his annual race. It was a great year. I knew I was going to be in Aspen for a long time.

After the season was over, I drove to June Lake to visit Wolfy. We went climbing in Yosemite and talked about going to Canada in June to fish, camp and climb in the Canadian Rockies. From there, I went to Bear Valley Ski Area for the Spring Far West Ski Instructors Convention. That year I didn't have to take an exam. I skied with Spyder Sabich who lived in Aspen, ski raced professionally and basically just relaxed and enjoyed the party.

I drove to Southern California to sell my Porsche. I was convinced that it just didn't make sense to own a sports car in a ski resort. I then flew back to Denver for my sister Sandy's wedding to Jimmy Ibbotson of the Nitty Gritty Dirt Band. She had only met him six months earlier in Aspen. The wedding was at Mom's in June. Wolfy was invited too, so we planned our trip through Canada.

Between the time that I had seen Wolfy in June Lake and Sandy's wedding, he had rescued a prairie falcon while fishing in the Owens River Valley just south of June Lake. Something had happened to the falcon's mother and he and his brother were alone in the nest and would have died had Wolfy and a friend of his not rescued the birds. Wolfy brought one of the falcons to Denver with intentions of raising it, training it to hunt and then releasing it back into the wild where he had found it.

I bought a Chevy Blazer so Wolfy, the falcon who we now called Pahono (from the Paiute Indian language meaning friend), and I loaded up in the blazer for a six-week-road trip through Canada. Wolfy knew that taking a falcon across the border into Canada would require some paperwork. He inquired about the necessary paperwork and was told he had to have a special license to even have a falcon in his possession. He took a class prior to our departure; an exam for a falconer's license. He wouldn't get the exam results for several weeks and even if he

Pahono just growing out of his baby feathers.
Prairie Falcon. Willie Waltner

passed it, it would take another week or so to receive the license. With a signed document from the professor of the class and a copy of the license application we decided to chance it and off we went not knowing what to expect. The one thing Wolfy did know was that he probably failed the test. It was an extremely difficult exam to pass and even veterinarians had trouble passing it.

We traveled up through Wyoming and stayed at Dave's ranch in Pinedale and then up through Montana, training Pahono to fly and hunt. We went through Glacier National Park toward the Canadian border. As we prepared to cross the border into Canada, we placed Pahono in a large closed box to keep him quiet. We had a 22-caliber squirrel gun that we used to kill small rodents to feed Pahono and a chunk of hashish, which we put in a couple of film canisters with all of Wolfy's camera equipment.

At the border everything went fine until the border patrol agent stuck his head in the window and said, "Have a nice trip." At that point Pahono went ballistic. He started squawking and carrying on. The border patrol agent wanted to know what was in the box. Wolfy and I looked at each other, got out of the car and very nicely showed the agent the bird and all of the paperwork that we had with us. We went into the office with Pahono while he made several phone calls. Things actually went pretty well. He searched the car rather thoroughly and found the squirrel gun. Instead of taking it away from us, knowing we were going to re-enter the U.S. from British Columbia (a border crossing a couple of hundred miles west of where we had entered), he wired the gun and tagged it so we couldn't fire it. He continued searching the car when he came upon the camera case. He opened it looked in a couple of film canisters with film in them, closed the camera case and let us continue on our trip.

Once we got going, Wolfy and I looked at each other. We were both sweating bullets. Wolfy said, "Let's pull over feed Pahono and have a couple of puffs." Wolfy figured out how to take the wire off the gun as soon as we left the border. We headed west through Banff and directly into the heart of the Canadian Rockies. What a beautiful place. We camped, fished and worked Pahono daily. By this time, we had the hang of what we were doing including Pahono. We kept the rodents we shot for Pahono in baggies in the cooler and only had to hunt for food a couple of times a week.

We met lots of people in the campgrounds we stayed in and everyone wanted to see Pahono. We had a perch that Pahono would sit on while we set up camp every evening. Every morning when we woke, we would have our coffee and take Pahono out to fly and feed him. One of us would hold him and the other, while wearing a leather glove, would get a hundred yards or so away with his food. We'd take the food from the bag and Pahono would fly to the food and eat.

We woke up one morning to a couple of inches of snow on the ground and still snowing lightly. Pahono loved the snow. We took him out to feed him and as he took off for his food, a lady nearby with a baby stroller, stopped to take out a plastic cap, unroll it and place it on her head to keep her hair dry. Pahono associated the plastic hair scarf with his food and went to land on the lady's head. She freaked out BIG TIME. We didn't blame her. Here comes a big bird out of nowhere and seemed to literally attack her! We got her settled down, explained what we were doing. She was okay with it. We were all a little freaked out, Pahono included.

We continued our trip through western Canada. One evening, while setting up camp, a couple came to check out Pahono. They invited us to have dinner with them. After dinner, they asked if we smoked marijuana. We said we did (we didn't have any, but we did have some hash). They had some pot but no rolling papers. They knew we had rolling papers because they saw that I rolled my own cigarettes ,"Sir Walter Raleigh." We smoked a joint, had a couple of puffs of hash, thanked them for dinner and went back to our camp to go to sleep.

We were about four days away from re-entering the U.S. We had had a great trip, fishing, camping and training Pahono. Wolfy was so pleased with Pahono's progress that he was actually looking forward to releasing him back into the Owens River Valley, where he had rescued him. That was still a couple of weeks away. We still had to get to Denver, where his car was, and then he had to drive back home to June Lake.

We arrived at a campground the night before we were to cross the border and took everything out of the car to consolidate all we could. As I was preparing dinner, I took the camp fuel and topped off the stoves and lantern. Not realizing it, I dripped fuel from the stove across the picnic table to where I placed the fuel container. I lit the stove to boil some water and the flame raced across the picnic table and into the fuel can. I grabbed the fuel can and threw it about ten feet away. In doing so, it lit our campsite on fire. People from all around us came with blankets and water to help put the fire out. I was still shaking and felt so stupid. I thought I was going to set western Canada on fire. Wolfy came up to me and said, "You know there's no way that fuel can was going to explode." I know that now!

The next morning before crossing the border, we packed up the car knowing that we were going to head straight back to Denver. We were ready for a hot shower, shave and a night's sleep in a real bed. Before we got to the border, Wolfy put the wire back on the gun so they couldn't tell we had tampered with it, and this time we put the little hash we had left inside the camera and wound it to 12. Wolfy put the camera around his neck. We couldn't find the rolling papers, but figured we had left them with the people we had dinner with. I was out of tobacco and had been for a couple of days.

The Border Patrol knew we were coming with falcon, gun and all (except the hash). They had been notified when we crossed into Canada several weeks prior and couldn't wait to see Pahono. They looked at the bird and checked the gun. We did all the necessary paperwork to re-enter the U.S. and were all ready to leave, but the patrol agent wanted to take one last look around. Wolfy was "taking pictures". The agent pulled the passenger seat forward to look in the back. My jacket was around the back of the passenger seat, and when the agent pulled it forward, the rolling papers fell out of the chest pocket of the jacket. They took the car apart. I tried to tell them that I rolled my own cigarettes, but without any tobacco they weren't buying it. About an hour later they were tired, we were tired of taking pictures and got in the car and drove off. Wolfy looked over at me and said, "Let's pull over, feed the bird and have a couple of puffs."

When we got back to Denver, Wolfy loaded up his van and Pahono and left for home, where he released the falcon back into the wild. As I left Denver to head back to Aspen for another season, I thought of my dog Amos, who I was missing. He had been stolen the spring before I left Aspen. I was really upset, knowing it took a while to get over losing a person, pet or anything that you truly loved.

I was thinking about Wolfy and Pahono and what a great trip we had traveling through Canada. All of a sudden, I just started laughing as I thought back to our adventure. Going into Canada we almost got busted for drugs, harboring an endangered species and a concealed weapon. Once we got into Canada, a woman almost died from a heart attack while being attacked by a wild bird, and I almost burned up Western Canada. Upon returning to the U.S., we almost got busted again for smuggling drugs across an international border with an endangered species. At both borders there were signs posted that read, "No Drugs Allowed." What a trip!!

Pahono watching us fishing for his dinner. Courtesy of Greg Smith

Yosemite Falls and Porsche from Hamburg. Courtesy of Greg Smith. Circa 1971

Climbing in Banff. Courtesy of Greg Smith. Circa 1971

Canadian Sunset. Courtesy of Greg Smith. 1971

Half Dome, Yosemite 1971. Courtesy of Greg Smith

"One That Got Away" Kathy Circa 1972

 Kathy
Winter 1971-1972

Last ski season I had roomed with a high school friend Greg Behr on the edge of town. Greg and I both had Mini Coopers in high school and at the end of the year we both decided to live together and get a place of our own. Greg stayed in Aspen that summer, while Wolfy and I gallivanted through Canada with a wild bird and hashish. Greg found a two-bedroom condo at the Mittendorf condominiums behind City Market. When I returned to Aspen, Indian summer was just beginning. It was gorgeous. The Aspen trees were just starting to change colors, reminding me of a bowl of Trix cereal.

I got work laying tile for a ski school supervisor, who had been my clinic leader in the hiring clinic the previous year. That's when I decided to make Aspen my home. The only obstacle before me was the same one everyone faced who pursued a seasonal career as a ski instructor. What would I do in the summer? I decided to worry about that when the time came.

The snow came early that year and it was good starting around Halloween time and continuing right through November. I met a beautiful girl watching rugby in Wagner Park and we really hit it off. Kathy worked two jobs, one in a meat market in town and the other as a receptionist at the Pokolodi Lodge in Snowmass Village. With me teaching at Snowmass, we found ourselves spending a lot of time together. She could ski a little, but I being a ski instructor remedied that in a hurry. We both worked hard and skied together whenever we could.

Kathy graduated from the University of Southern California and like most graduates she wanted to have some fun before getting married, settling down and having children. She lived with some of her college girlfriends about two blocks from where Greg and I had our condo. A couple of Kathy's friends from college, Mike Morgan and Rusty Jordan, who I got to know very well, showed up in early spring driving a 10-wheel blue panel truck used to haul produce, which they had converted into a motor home they christened The Blue Goose. Mike and Rusty were farmers from the Imperial Valley just outside of Brawley California.

I did a lot of powder skiing that winter. On powder mornings, I would meet up with my photographer friend, Butch Gilmartin. He would shoot photos of me on Snowmass Mountain for his portfolio. He took some amazing pictures. After our photo session, I would meet for ski school while he developed his film. We did this whenever we could. He sold quite a few of his photos around town. I knew this because I would see them everywhere in restaurants, ski shops and lodges. I think he did pretty well. I kept asking him when I was going to get a piece of the action? He took a great photo of me in uniform riding the Fanny Hill lift at Snowmass, while teaching a kids' group.

A lot of the ski instructors smoked back then. We used to throw our cigarette butts off the lift, until someone told us that it took 20 years for a cigarette butt to decompose. So we would get rid of the tobacco part and put the filters in a pocket to throw away at the end of the day. I didn't like my uniform smelling like cigarette butts, so I rolled my own, "Sir Walter Raleigh."

On that particular day, riding the Fanny Hill lift, Butch took a picture of me smoking while riding with a kid in my class. He made a poster of the picture and titled it, "Ski Stoned". That poster hung in our locker room for the rest of the ski season. I thought I would never hear the end of it. Thank God we all had a good sense of humor. It wasn't there the next year and I never heard another word about it. That was a good thing!!

You gotta get your nose in it to like it. Courtesy Butch Gilmartin

When spring came and Aspen closed for the season, we would go skiing in Vail, Breckenridge or Crested Butte. Those areas would stay open a week or more longer depending on the snow. That was our spring party, a little road trip to a nearby resort.

Kathy and I loaded up the Blazer and left Aspen during what everyone called, "mud season". We went to Denver to see my mom, then to California to visit Kathy's parents in Pasadena. We'd shop and go to the beach, which was always overcast that time of year, but it was nice to get out of Aspen and relax. After we left Kathy's parents, we went to Brawley to visit Michael and see his farming operation. He farmed about six hundred acres at the time, but had plans to expand. We also went over to visit Rusty just outside of Blithe on the Colorado River. We water-skied, played in the 90° heat, barbecued great food and drank a lot of beer.

About the time we arrived back in Aspen the trees were starting to turn green, mud season was finally over and the ground was beginning to reveal its native grasses. It was so beautiful and nice to now call Aspen my home. Kathy and I found our own little apartment right at the base of Aspen

Mountain. It was perfect for us, one large bedroom, bath, small living area with a kitchen and a large deck all furnished. Kathy got a job at Cooper Street Pier as a cocktail waitress and I kind of floated around doing odd jobs, tile work or anything I could find.

Pow Pow Snowmass. Circa 1971. Courtesy Butch Gilmartin

Pepsi and Aspen Villa
Winter 1972-1973

Finally winter had arrived and I could go do what I did best, teach skiing. Kathy's job was working out great. She loved it and did well with tips. It also gave her lots of time during the day to ski. She got quite good at it and really enjoyed it. I started ski racing again, primarily ski school races. We were the Aspen Ski School Team and would go to Vail and other resorts close by to compete as a team. We did well and usually won.

By now, the ski school director felt I was more valuable teaching adults and private lessons rather than kids. They paid based upon certification level, which put me in the top pay category. Since the adult ski school and private lessons cost more than a day at the kid's ski school, the company got more bang for their buck by moving me to adult and private lessons. From that time on, I taught a lot of private lessons. The bigger the group classes became, the more value guests would find in one-on-one attention and the tips certainly reflected that.

Kathy didn't have the time to go on a long trip that Spring, so we did our usual spring ski trip to Vail, saw my mom in Denver and got back to Aspen in mid-spring. Kathy needed to be back early to cover for some of her co-workers at the restaurant, to give them an extended spring break. Once again, I found myself doing whatever I could to help pay the rent. I found work with one of my ski school friends doing a little landscaping. I liked being outside planting trees, mowing yards, fixing sprinkler leaks and broken heads. I also helped Peter and Mary Anne get their house on Cemetery Lane ready to sell because they were about ready to build a house in Starwood.

Julie Bard, a girl I taught with at Snowmass and who lived upstairs, came running into our apartment one day, telling me to come with her to audition for a television commercial at the golf course. I thought to myself, "Yeah right" but I went along to see what was going on. The crew was shooting two commercials for Pepsi Cola. One was a backpacking and camping spot with a little mountain climbing involved and the other was an annual fictitious company outing spot with food, games and a lot of Pepsi.

Julie was cast for one of the spots and I was put in both. Filming was going to start in about five or six days; as soon as the right backpacking location was found. The assistant director asked me if I knew of a good place to shoot that wasn't on private property and close to town. I suggested looking up Independence Pass. It was close, beautiful, with a lot of places to do a little rock climbing and backpacking.

Knowing I was going to be in the rock climbing spot, I drove up the pass to practice a little bouldering and repelling. I was carrying a backpack with some climbing equipment up the "Grado Wall" to practice some repelling. I took a big step and tore something in my left knee. It wasn't that big of a deal at the time. There was a little fluid in it the next day, but that wasn't going to stop me from being a movie star. Independence Pass was chosen for that commercial. The other location was shot on the Roaring Fork River just below Woody Creek. It was a lot of fun and very interesting. I got to know the assistant director, Thom and his wife Herad. They became good friends and Kathy and I had them over for dinner a few times.

In the meantime, my knee continued to worsen. It finally got to the point where it would lock up on me just rolling over in bed. I knew that if I was going to ski that winter, I would need surgery. As it turned out, I ended up with a serious infection after surgery which kept me in the hospital for thirty days. Just prior to my knee surgery, I had inherited $10,000 from my great grandmother. I was supposed to receive it when I turned 21, but it got tied up in probate. Using that money as a down payment and Dave co-signing the note, I purchased an Aspen Villa townhouse.

It was a pretty big place, 1700 square feet with three bedrooms, 1-1/2 baths and a large unfinished basement. My two best friends moved in with me for the winter and we split the mortgage. Interestingly enough, the townhouse was right next door to the first house I had lived in with Jamie when I first moved to town. I moved into it the following Christmas and Kathy kept the little apartment with her best friend from college who had recently moved to Aspen.

Michael and Rusty
Winter 1973-1974

I was unable to teach that winter, but the head supervisor, Jan Johansson, at Snowmass put me in charge of the private lesson desk. It worked out fine. I assigned all private lessons that year and was able to ski a little by the end of the season. With a little beer and Norwegian aquavit liquor in me, I was able to do a few flips at the end of the season party.

Kathy and I went to Crested Butte for a little spring skiing. We left Aspen in April during mud season, to visit our families, stopping first at Rusty's to water ski on the Colorado River and then to Brawley to visit Michael. While in southern California visiting Kathy's parents, we spent time at Thom and Herad's house in the Hollywood hills. Kathy and I enjoyed our spring vacations away from Aspen. It was a good time to reflect, see good friends who didn't live in Aspen, and just relax and thaw out. When we got back to Aspen Kathy continued working at Cooper Street Pier. I went to Denver to help Mom out and move my belongings from the Denver house into my new villa in Aspen.

Mike and me. Sea of Cortez

Rusty giving me his English taxi.

Party on Aspen Mountain. Circa 1974. Courtesy Edgar Boyles.

Mountain Dew
Summer 1974

I was getting my villa in order and it was beginning to feel more and more like home. My two roommates, Scott and Dan, both had small businesses. Scott had started a sprinkler system business, and Dan, who had previously worked summers in Oregon as a smoke jumper, had decided to stay in Aspen full time. As an avid river rat, he started up a small rafting company floating tourists down the river. Wolfy came out to stay that summer to help Scott with his sprinkler system venture.

Knowing a little about landscaping, I helped Scott and Wolfy install sprinkler systems. It turned into quite a lucrative business for Scott. By that time he had acquired the nickname of "Wheels", most likely given to him by Wolfy. We all worked hard. Wheels would bid the jobs, then drive to Ogden, Utah to pick up materials from a company he had worked for a couple of summers earlier. Then Wolfy and I would install the systems.

We had a good sprinkler system, which seemed to flow quite nicely. We put them in all over town including large residential homes on Red Mountain, Starwood, the West End and commercial systems in Snowmass for condos, hotels and businesses. We did several large parcels for horse properties that required separate small reservoirs with pumps, which would feed the different zones.

About midway through the summer, I received a call from Thom, my assistant director friend in Hollywood. He asked me if I could do some pre-production work for a couple of Mountain Dew commercials that he was going to direct, hopefully in Aspen. Aspen was starting to become a little Mecca for the Hollywood crowd. They loved coming to Aspen to work and it proved to have all the necessary components

A "selfie" of Thom and me location scouting. Circa 1974. Courtesy Thom Anable.

in a relatively small place to adequately fulfill their needs, such as location, talent, transportation, lodging and most importantly a community that embraced their presence. Many in the movie industry had been coming to Aspen for a while now to get away from city life. It was a place where they could be left alone, relax and not worry about people bothering them.

Thom had sent me some storyboards asking me to search for appropriate locations. His preference was on forest service property rather than private property. I looked into hotel rooms, places to hold castings, rehearsals and pretty much everything necessary to film a commercial without having to bring Hollywood to town. Thom was planning to film two commercials. One was a river sequence complete with tubing, rafting, canoeing and a little hiking. The other was a horseback outing with waterfalls, a little fishing and some trail riding in the mountains.

The locations for the commercials in Aspen were a no-brainer. Having the Roaring Fork River, Independence Pass, the Grottos, the Maroon Bells, with all their beauty and splendor, waterfalls, mountains and of course horses everywhere, made my search easy. This was a great job opportunity for me. I was able to do all the logistics and pre-production work as well as to be casted in one or both commercials.

I was cast in the river and hiking commercial. We filmed it on the Roaring Fork River just west of town and at the Grottos, up Independence Pass. We shot the hotbox scene where the actor sits on a box relishing the product, in this case, gulp down a Mountain Dew, at Maroon Lake. Mountain Dew wasn't my drink of choice. It was a relatively new soda and I personally hadn't acquired a taste

One Take Tommy! Whew! Circa 1974. Maroon Bells. Courtesy of Howard Freeman at Slidemaster

for it. It also contained a lot of caffeine, so it was important for me to try to get this in one take otherwise I would be buzzing around more than I already did!

I sat on the "hot box" while the director said "Action". I managed to pour the whole bottle down in one big gulp. Of course it backed up a little and came out of my nose, but that's the kind of stuff the advertising agency wants. Fortunately, we were able to shoot that in one take. Evidently it worked out well for them—when the commercial aired that take closed the end of the sixty-second spot.

Maroon Bells. Courtesy Greg Smith.

Ski Racing and a Really Good Songwriter
Winter 1974-1975

Snowmass Ski School (uniform of the future). Circa 1800s - ha ha!

When winter came I was really looking forward to ski racing. There had been a slightly different format introduced by U.S. women's ski coach Bob Beattie and with the likes of Spider Sabich and a few other world cup names, Bob put together a dual format similar to head-to-head racing at a horse track. Two racers would attack a course head-to-head and the time differential was collected. The racers would then go back to the top switch courses and race again. The slower racer on the first run would have to beat his opponent by more than the margin of the first run to advance to the next round. It proved to be a great spectator sport. Big jumps were built into the course that racers had to negotiate without blowing out of their respective course. Each course was side-by-side and not too far apart. It was exciting to watch.

Between teaching a lot of private lessons and a little ski racing, my winter was shaping up to be a good one. At a place like Aspen you never know who you're going to meet next. Early in the season I skied with John and Anne Denver. John played guitar and sang at well-known eateries in Snowmass when he was home. He was a really good singer/songwriter. I enjoyed skiing with him and his wife, who took several ski lessons with me. She was a delightful young lady who picked up skiing rather quickly. We skied together often that year while John was being whisked into the limelight of stardom.

My roommate Wheels also taught with me at Snowmass and was an area consultant for Rossignol Ski Company. We skied a lot together and would help the pro racers whenever they were in town, schlepping their skis around, and giving them oxygen when they finished their run, before going back up for another one. Rossignol had their own pro racer technician, who traveled with them from venue to venue each week. The racers themselves would fly from place to place, generally taking a pair of training skis while they waited for the technician to show up with the van full of race skis for the next race. Wheels and I thought that would be a great job serving the racers, taking care of their skis and driving back and forth across the country from race to race.

The ski school races I competed in adopted this format and it was exciting to participate and complete head to head. Our ski school team adapted successfully to this format generally doing well against other ski schools around the state. There were a lot of ski instructors employed on all three mountains, though Highlands was privately owned at the time. We still had an abundance of talented pros to choose from for the team.

The warm weather version of that uniform (quite the look).

Spoony's Lunch Wagon
Summer 1975

Kathy and I took a short road trip to California to visit Thom and Herad, our farming friends, and Kathy's parents. We arrived back in Aspen while mud season was in full swing. Wolfy had left early the previous winter, so Wheels and I got a jump-start on his sprinkler system business. We had all of his clients up and running before summer hit. We fixed waterlines that had broken during the winter freeze and replaced damaged heads that plow trucks hit near driveways and sidewalks. It seemed all of this maintenance was going to be ongoing, which gave us a sense of job security.

Wheels picked up several new accounts right off the bat. As people recognized the value in water savings and the convenience of no longer having to haul hoses, Wheels picked up more and more accounts. I enjoyed it because it enabled Wolfy to come back and work with us. Wheels got so busy he hired a couple of guys who worked with us teaching skiing at Snowmass.

Meanwhile, Mom had bought a lot in Starwood close to Peter's, the guy she had dated in Colorado Springs while I was growing up. She rented a house within walking distance from my villa on Cemetery Lane, where she stayed with Patty and David. She was building her new house in Starwood, which wouldn't be finished until the following summer. Not much gets done in the winter in Aspen, unless it is ski related.

With Wheels having plenty of help by now, I was thinking more and more about starting my own small business. My brother Willie had started a business with a college friend that was premature for its time, so they shut it down and he moved to Aspen to pursue something new. I bought a catering truck in Colorado Springs and Willie helped me get my little catering company-on-wheels started. I decided to call my company, "Spoony's Lunch Wagon", after my old June Lake nickname. I wasn't really the spoiled rich kid, but it was fitting. In any event, I decided to have flyers with the Bill of Fare menus printed up so I could place them around various construction sites where the workers would expect me to show up.

I went to a new printing business in town called Aspen State Teachers College. Don't ask me why they named it that. In the mid-70s the town was full of twisted people, who generally had fun names for whatever services they were offering. I walked in and the place looked like a student union similar to any college campus. A guy named Slats Cabbage helped me. I never asked him if that was his real name or not. I picked up one of their brochures and when I got home I discovered the place was promoting themselves as a college, complete with curriculum and athletic gear consisting of hats T-shirts and sweats all with their A.S.T.C. logo. I thought it was hysterical and showed the brochure to Willie. He thought it would be funny to send Dave the information, along with a pair of gym shorts, to try to get him to buy me a scholarship for college since he had been upset that I had never gone.

Moey checking out the lunch wagon. 1975

I went back to get my menus and pick up some stuff to send to Dave thinking that would be the end of it, but about a week or so later I received a card from Dave with a check made out to Aspen State Teachers College for $20.00. In the memo line of the check it said, "Send me a baseball cap!" The card said, "Thanks for the shorts, but I think the PhD you got in June Lake for shoveling all that snow suited your career just fine."

That summer I would get up early in the morning and prepare the truck for the day. I'd get donuts in town from Little Cliff's Bakery, pick up my soft drinks from the Coca-Cola truck at City Market, and get shaved ice from the ice rink in town to refrigerate my truck. I made my rounds to the rafting company, meeting the tourists on the river and construction sites around town.

At noontime, I had several stops with sandwiches I had picked up at the In And Out House on Main Street across from Carl's Pharmacy. When the afternoons would roll back around, I hit the building sites again and a couple of school bus stops where the kids would buy soda and candy bars after school. It worked out great because I would be done by 3:30 p.m., I'd clean the truck, gas it up and do my paperwork. Then I'd check on Mom and play softball at Wagner Park with Wheels, Wolfy, and a lot of my friends.

We played on John Curiel's team, the Wildcats. He was the local hairdresser in town, one step above a barbershop. He cut a lot of celebrities' hair. People from LA would actually wait to have John cut or style their hair when they came out on holiday.

Thom and the film crew came out to film another spot for Mountain Dew, but I wasn't cast for that commercial as I had been the last couple of years.

With softball over, our team turned its sights towards flag football.
It was like playing in a bowl of Trix with all those colors.

The consensus was that my "mug" had been seen associated with soft drinks enough. I was still able to help with the pre-production locations and overall logistics for the commercials.

Rossignol Consultant
Winter 1975-1976

Wheels went to work full time as a technical representative for the Rossignol Ski Company and hired me to be their Aspen area consultant. I was in charge of pro sales for all ski professionals at all four mountains in Aspen.

Curt Chase, the director of the ski school, had transferred me to Buttermilk for several reasons. One reason being, I was closer to Aspen Mountain. That way if they were about to run out of ski instructors, he could pull me from Buttermilk. With a short five-minute drive I could be at Ajax ready for work. As an area consultant, now I was more centrally located to handle my duties for all the ski professionals in Aspen. It was relatively easy to put three hundred plus pros on Rossignol skis each year. They were by far the most popular skis and Rossignol knew the importance of having their presence on as many pros as possible at the beginning of each season. All the ski reps for the different companies would hold what was called a 'flex session', where pros would come to purchase whatever they needed for the upcoming season including boots, poles, skis and clothing.

I enjoyed teaching at Buttermilk. I would arrive early and stay late to run gates (slalom and giant slalom) on a run below the Tiehack lift called Ego Hill. It was a great place to train because the hill had a good pitch and was accessed by a short lift, which would bring you back to the top in seven minutes. There was also a small restaurant at the bottom and a parking lot. All of this was about five minutes from where I lived.

That Christmas my ski lesson booking was with Beverly and Vidal Sassoon. Well needless to say, my friend and hairdresser John Curiel, whom I played baseball with in the summers, would have killed to meet them. Just by happenstance, one day when Beverly and Vidal were having lunch, John stopped by. I introduced both of them to John and he joined us for lunch. From that day on I was John's best friend, which worked out great for me. I didn't pay for another hair cut as long as he cut hair in Aspen.

I really liked ski racing and wanted to compete on the professional tour. I trained hard and traveled outside the Aspen area to Vail, Winter Park, Sun Valley, Idaho and even Heavenly Valley in California to try and qualify for the tour. Qualifying was held on Thursdays at each venue. A leading pro racer would set a time on either a slalom or giant slalom course and the racers trying to qualify would have to be within five percent of his time. I'd skied well each time, but not quite good enough, a couple hundredths of a second out. It was close enough that I would try week in and week out.

The weeks that I didn't travel to qualify for the pro tour, I'd compete in a satellite tour within a three-state region. On that tour I skied in the top ten. Celestial Seasonings and Coors Brewery put on a race every Saturday at Aspen Highlands. I would always race there if I wasn't competing somewhere else.

At some point that season I received a call from John Russell, a sports photographer whom I had met several times over the course of the winter. He photographed a lot of ski racers on the pro tour. He called in April and needed to photograph some racers for print advertising for Rossignol. Aspen had closed for the season, so we went over to Copper Mountain with a higher elevation for a two-day shoot. John had perfect conditions to film. It snowed several inches each night with crystal blue skies every day, rather common during springtime in the Rockies, so he was able to get some great pictures. I appeared in a Rossignol poster and a couple of ads in Ski and Skiing Magazines that next season.

Grand Canyon
Summer 1976

My spring trip was going to be one that I would remember for the rest of my life. My roommate Dan and several of our rafting friends applied for a raft trip in the Grand Canyon. The permits were drawn lottery style. We were very lucky to have been picked. We scheduled an eighteen-day trip, starting at Lees Ferry below the Glen Canyon Dam. In the late sixties. the dam had been built creating Lake Powell, a stretch that ended in Peach Springs, Nevada, just east of Lake Mead.

The trip got underway after a long shuttle of cars. From our put-in to our take-out, a trip like this required a lot of preparation without any conveniences along the way. We'd have to bring everything we'd need for eighteen days and take out all our trash, leaving nothing behind. We packed everything in ammo cans and waterproof enclosures, from our food to our sleeping bags. It was an unbelievable trip from start to finish. For eighteen days the only human life that existed was with the eighteen friends who were on the trip. Remarkably, we all got along with very few anxious moments. Thank God for beer! We had a lot of it. It traveled in gunnysacks tied behind each raft in the cold Colorado River and everyone had his or her share of drugs.

Kathy and Sue (Dan's fiancée) met us in Havasupai, an Indian reservation two-thirds of the way through the canyon. We hiked up the stream from the bottom of the canyon to the reservation to meet them. On the way back Dan sprained his ankle and spent a lot of time soaking it in the beautiful aqua blue stream. You couldn't drink the water because it was contaminated with Giardia, but somehow Dan got enough of it in him to get sick. We ended up spending one extra day. By then Dan was just well enough to oar the raft through Lava Falls rapid, which is the second largest drop in the Colorado River. The biggest is right before Glenwood Springs, just outside of Aspen.

When we arrived in Peach Springs a park and recreation officer met us. We were one day late and had two extra people. I personally didn't deal with the officer. One of the organizers of our trip dealt with him, which was probably a good thing. Nineteen days of river negotiating with the same group of people made it difficult to adjust to the real world. It took me a day or two to completely readjust.

When I returned to Aspen, I fired up my catering truck and continued with my business. Later that summer, I was having trouble so I sold it to a woman who already had a catering company and wanted to expand. I also got involved with a little ranching. I loved it. It reminded me of the time I spent with Dave at the ranch in Wyoming. I rode bucking horses at the Snowmass Rodeo on Thursdays and in Rifle at the Garfield County Fairgrounds. I also went to work for a friend, who I had raced with, installing zero clearance fireplaces and screens. His family owned a store in town called The Burning Log.

Once again, I was called upon to help with the production of a Ford automobile commercial. I was quickly learning how to take advantage of small moneymaking jobs just to make ends meet. I put the fireplace duties on hold for a week while I helped with the Ford commercial. By now I knew the necessary steps involved in production work. This commercial went smoothly, other than one small glitch. We needed a dirt road wide enough to drive six cars side-by-side, basically the whole Ford line for that model year. The place I found to shoot the driving sequence was the county road above Snowmass Village. That was some road. The area for the company picnic was a ranch near Woody Creek, near where we had filmed the Pepsi commercial a few years back. Neither place was a problem to set up.

The morning of the shoot the caterer took the advertising agency executives to check out the picnic spot. While on the way, the executives felt they could shoot the driving sequence on a road closer to the picnic spot. They didn't realize it was private property and hadn't obtained permission. Well, all hell broke loose as they set up and prepared to film. The owners of the private driveway showed up and demanded that they move. I had just shown up on the road above Snowmass Village wondering where they were. Once I found them, I was able to talk to the people who owned the private road and smooth things out. The commercial ended up going over budget, but at that point taking another day to relocate the film crew would have been very costly.

Dan, Susan, Kathy & me. Lava Falls, Grand Canyon.

Rossignol Technical Representative
Winter 1976-1977

The winter of 1976-1977 will go down in history as the year of the great Colorado snow draught. It didn't snow until mid-January, so the lifts and ski areas didn't open until then. Wheels took a position as sales rep for the Garmont Ski Boot Company. It was a great opportunity with a lot of growth potential. It opened the door for me, as I was able to move into his position with Rossignol Ski Company as technical rep.

My territory was southern Wyoming, Colorado and New Mexico. I was given a van to drive, a salary and a full expense account. I traveled to all of the Rossignol dealers in my region. I taught ski shop mechanics about our various ski models and how to maintain and mount different ski bindings on our product line. I still serviced the Rossignol race team and maintained their equipment whenever they raced in my territory. As I spent more time on technical responsibilities, I spent less time on snow training and racing myself. That nagging knee injury I had suffered several years back made ski racing less of a reality.

I spent a lot of time demoing skis to all types of ski professionals. One of my main objectives was to put lots of skis on the snow. I had area consultants in all of the major ski resorts in my territory, which made it easy to create pro sales at a professional discount.

Working for Rossignol added a few extra months to my winter season. I would start in October introducing our new ski product line and train shop mechanics. I would then work with the resorts once they opened, then finish the year at different race camps in the spring. I also had four or five months of summer to ranch and help with any production work that would come up.

Close your mouth and drive!

Sea of Cortez
Summer 1977

I spent quite a bit of time with my friend Michael at his farm in the
Imperial Valley. We water skied and flew around his farmland checking the
crops from the air in his Cessna 180 tail dragger. Michael was a really good
pilot, but wouldn't release his draft records to the F.A.A. They refused to
grant him a flying license. It may have had something to do with insurance;
I never really understood. I think he had polio as a child and one leg was a
couple of inches shorter than the other, classifying him as 4-F and exempting
him from military service, which may have been why.

We also spent a lot of time fishing and exploring in the Sea of Cortez
on his boat, between Baja, California and mainland Mexico. He spoke
fluent Spanish because all of his farm employees were migrant workers from
Mexico. I loved the Sea of Cortez. We would put the boat in at San Felipe
and travel as far as the Bay of Los Angeles, fishing and exploring the Mid
Drift Islands. One island was a bird sanctuary and nesting place for all of the
saltwater bird species in Baja.

Mulegé Baja Mexico

Midrift Islands, Sea of Cortez, Circa 1976

Michael keeping a close eye out for the whalesharks.

Michael Landon's Double
Winter 1977-1978

It took a little time to fully understand my job description with Rossignol, however by now I was pretty comfortable with my job. I did get a little tired of driving from Ruidosa, New Mexico in the southeast part of the state to Laramie and Cheyenne, Wyoming and all points in between. When I got home, I would have just enough time to empty my suitcase, clean my clothes, pay my bills, catch up on my expense account to get reimbursed, and pack a new bag for the road again. The good part was I spent most of my time in Colorado. There were always promotional activities happening where I would show up to demo skis and show Rossignol presence on snow.

Through my answering service, I received a call from Thom, my director friend. He was shooting a Kodak commercial and needed my assistance. I contacted the Nordica ski boot rep that also worked closely on these events. We both showed up in Vail and outfitted the people involved. As it turned out, Michael Landon the star of the commercial, didn't ski and his stunt

My best Michael Landon "look". 1977. Photo by John Russell

85

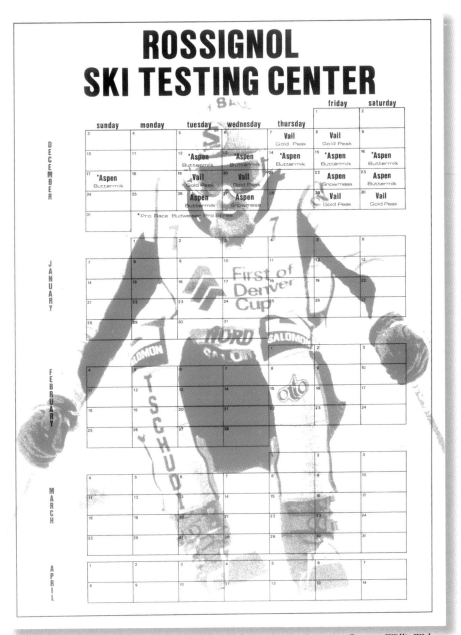

Sample Schedule for New Demo Program. Courtesy Willie Waltner

double couldn't get the hang of it soon enough for the filming. Thom asked me to come and meet the ad agency personnel and director of the shoot to see if I had any ideas on how to get it done. They were a little desperate since all the people in this business are with budgets and all. I came in to meet the director, sat down and began discussing the problem he faced. I really wasn't much help.

The next thing I knew he put a hat, goggles and ski parka on me looked at the ad agency director and asked, "What do you think?"

He said, "Let's go with it." The director proceeded to tell me not to cut my hair. Two days later Michael Landon's stunt double still couldn't ski well enough to accomplish what they wanted, so they cast me as Landon's stunt double skiing in the commercial. I didn't look like Michael Landon but the director felt confident he could pull off the shot if my face was covered with a hat and goggles exposing my long black wavy hair.

That spring I went to Mammoth for the Rossignol sponsored race camps, which lasted through May. I met with the Rossignol executives who asked me if I could create a new demo program and test it between Vail and Aspen for the next season. I agreed to give it a try.

 ## Whale Sharks
Summer 1978

When the race camps ended, I went to my friend Mike's farm where we loaded up the boat and traveled to San Felipe. From there, we put the boat in and took off to Gonzaga Bay to film some more of Baja and hopefully ride the Whale Sharks, which migrated to the bay, along with the plankton they fed on. Whale Sharks are the biggest fish in the ocean and aren't the least bit interested in harming people. I spent the rest of the summer putting together the new demo program for Rossignol and married Kiki Cutter in late November. Kiki was an American World Cup and Olympic competitor whose claim to fame was winning slalom in Oslo, becoming the first American to win a World Cup event, in 1968.

Rossignol Promo Film
Winter 1978 - 1979

The demo program for Rossignol was very successful. As a pilot program set up for just Vail and Aspen, the two largest ski resorts in Colorado, it seemed to please not only the consumer who participated by demoing the product, but the dealers' sales were up as well. The concept worked so well it was implemented by not only Rossignol, but by other equipment manufacturers worldwide. I still see the program today when I travel to different ski resorts. The manufacturer reps show up slope side with their vans full of skis. They demo not only to the professionals at the resort, but for the skiing public as well.

Rossignol Ski Company contacted Bisch Fox Productions in New York, the same company they had hired to do the advertising campaign with John Russell in 1977. They wanted to make a promotional ski film to introduce the new product line in 1980 for the reception center at the 1980 Winter Olympic Games in Lake Placid, New York. John Douglas, the promotional coordinator for Rossignol Ski Company, had them contact me to help orchestrate the logistics.

Sweetheart with her foal a year after Michael gave her to us as a gift. 1981.

We shot the piece in Aspen that spring. I put together the cast locations and storyboards and produced and directed the short film. Other than some of the language used in the film, which seemed a little redundant, everyone seemed satisfied with the outcome and the video. It was sent to all of the dealers throughout the country as a sales tool for their respective ski shops.

At this point, I was satisfied with everything I had accomplished in my ski career and wanted to explore other opportunities and avenues. I decided to get my real estate license, sold my villa in Aspen, bought a fifteen acre ranch with my farming friend Mike, and moved to Carbondale.

Mike gave Kiki and me a thoroughbred racehorse for a wedding present and had it sent from his farm in Brawley, California to our new ranch. I went to Wyoming to my stepfather's ranch and picked up Wizard, my sister Sandy's Quarter horse, to make our little ranch complete. Kiki and I each had a horse to ride. Horses are social animals and do better in pairs.

Kiki and her new Saab. Courtesy Dick Zeder. Circa 1980.

EIGHTIES & NINETIES

Winter Olympics Lake Placid
Winter 1979-1980

Miracle-on-Ice

I traveled to Lake Placid for the 1980 Winter Olympics to help John Douglas and Kiki with the Rossignol Reception Center. It was an exciting time to say the least. I was fortunate enough to see some of the events. Bob Beattie (aka Beats), Kiki's ex-husband, got early-round hockey tickets for his wife Cheryl (my high school girlfriend). Now how ironic was that! Beats wanted us to go together to see the USA play Sweden (I believe it ended in a tie). Cheryl and I also saw the U.S. beat the Czechoslovakian team to advance to the medal round against Russia.

The electricity in the air at Lake Placid was like nothing I had ever seen. Russia had beaten the U.S. team two weeks earlier in Madison Square Garden, but this game was to be the highlight of the Lake Placid Olympic Games. Unfortunately, Beats couldn't get tickets for Cheryl and me to go. They were impossible to come by, so I watched it on the big screen T.V. with John at the reception center. I will never forget pacing back and forth in front of that T.V. the last ten minutes of the game. Main Street in Lake Placid was like a ghost town during the game. If you couldn't be at the hockey arena in town you were somewhere watching it on T.V.

When the game ended, I never experienced anything like it. The streets of Lake Placid filled with people carrying American flags. I thought the people were going to come through the windows of the recreation center. It was absolutely crazy. I returned home from Lake Placid two days before my thirtieth birthday and my hair was still standing straight up!

Kentucky Derby
Summer 1980

That spring, Mike and his fiancé took Kiki and me to the Kentucky Derby. Mike's mom was married to Dr. Alex Harthill, the foremost thoroughbred veterinarian in the country. They lived in Louisville. This was the year Genuine Risk won. I sat next to Jack Klugman at a dinner hosted by Mike's mom the night before the race. Jack had a horse racing in the Derby.

It was a filly by the name of none other than Jacqueline Klugman. The horse showed third place and I won $48.00 on a $2.00 bet. The Derby was a great time.

Coming home, I was thinking how lucky I was to have floated for 21 days through the Grand Canyon, experience one of the greatest hockey games ever at

Me, Michael and Deirdre at the Kentucky Derby.

the Olympic Games in Lake Placid, and sit in one of the best boxes at the Kentucky Derby. I had just turned 30 years old. Life was good.

The real estate market was in a slump, so I was looking for anything to help supplement what little income I had at the time. The film "Jaws" was about to be released. I really wanted to try to put together a film about Baja and the Whale Sharks. I thought a documentary dealing with how docile Whale Sharks were would help put people at ease knowing that all sharks aren't out to eat people.

So Mike and I went back down to Baja and took some more photos and fished. I had

Michael's mom helping me with my racing form.

enough information to make a presentation to any outdoor sport program. I met with a cameraman, who in turn gave my proposal to a producer with American Sportsman. They did end up making a documentary on Whale Sharks, but I was never asked to be involved.

Cheryl Ladd and Oil Shale
Winter 1980-1981

Later that fall the same cameraman was filming a documentary with Cheryl Ladd. They were tagging mountain lions and monitoring their behavior in Rifle, Colorado just outside of Glenwood Springs, at the Puma Paw Ranch. He offered me a job as his assistant. It took several trips to get all the necessary footage. On our final trip, a make-it or break-it outing, it all came together. The dogs treed a puma. The wildlife officers tranquilized, tagged and released it back into the wild to monitor its activity. It wasn't quite as easy as it may sound, but it was way cool to be part of that production.

Being at the mercy of the mountain lion during this production, we had a lot of down time so I would cruise to Rifle to look around. Only 1-1/2 hours from Aspen, it was booming with oil shale production. I was selling real estate, so it made sense. With the domestic oil production lagging in the U.S., Union Oil was extracting oil from the shale in Rifle and the surrounding areas — and there was a lot of it. There were some jewelry stores in Rifle that would take the rock and polish it up nicely and make jewelry out of it. They did quite well selling it as souvenirs to the tourists and people in the oil industry.

Of course I got this idea that I could cash in on this natural resource that was covering the ground everywhere. Between Rifle and the small town of Parachute was an operation called Parahoe. I arranged to talk to the head foreman of the mine and told him I was visiting the area and had some dealings with Shell Oil (thinking of my friend Jim who worked with Shell Oil in Houston) and wanted a small tour of the operation. He put a hard hat on me and took me everywhere. There were big dump trucks that would drive up into a mountain range that spanned from Rifle all the way to Grand Junction. They would load up the trucks with huge boulders of fresh oil shale and drive them to a small train station next to Interstate-70. From there the trains would haul the shale to have the oil extracted from the rock.

When the dump trucks brought the big rocks down to be loaded on the trains, pieces would fall off onto the road. I asked the foreman what they would do with the scattered pieces? He said, "Nothing, some knucklehead comes and picks it up and does whatever with it." I asked if I could take some of the small rocks and he told me to help myself. I became that knucklehead!

That was the start of my new small company I called, "Rifle Rock Originals". I would take the rock and cut it into slabs with a diamond blade wet tile saw. Then I would sand the slabs with a belt sander I borrowed from a ski shop that was used to tune skis. I would polish the shale slabs and put a coat of polyurethane on them. It was beautiful looking like petrified wood or agate. I'd dress them up with little oil cans, oil derricks, anything oil related and sell them in gift stores.

Jim arranged for me to meet with a couple of oil executives at Shell Oil in Houston to introduce my line of products. They all loved them, but rather than deal with me directly they suggested I go to the Dallas Merchandise Mart where they sold oil related products to all the retailers in Texas. Here I was this 30-year-old ski instructor with a legal sized brief case on wheels carting around 100 pounds of oil shale samples with no clue what I was doing. The people at the Merchandise Mart were very nice to me and loved my products. They, in turn, put me in touch with a company in Tulsa, Oklahoma that manufactured nothing but oil-related gifts.

I jumped on a commuter flight from D.F.W. to Tulsa, Oklahoma. There the owner of the company met me at the airport. Carl was a welder by trade, sporting tattoos and earrings, and he looked like a welder. He made some of the coolest stuff. Lamps with oil derrick stands, which were seen on the set of "Dallas" in J.R. Ewing's office and the grasshopper-type-oil rigs that American Express Catalog had on their front cover one year, just to name a few. He liked the whole idea of oil shale, had heard of it but had never seen it. He was surprised at how beautiful the stuff was. For the next two years I supplied him with the slabs, which were all different. He would take them and put his creations on the slabs to appear as if they were extracting the oil directly from the shale.

During this time the real estate market was still pretty slow and Kiki was doing promotional events for the ski industry. She skied in a Legends Race in Beaver Creek and one of the executives on her team was president of Saab Motors U.S.A. He was an avid skier and knew of Kiki's history. He offered Kiki a Saab, which she took of course. It was delivered to her through Bighorn Motors in Glenwood Springs, Colorado. We got to know the owner Dick Zeder quite well. He used Kiki for some promotional events and offered me a job selling Saabs and Toyotas.

My car sales job only lasted about a year. In that time, I had learned a lot about people and their needs. With skiing I was able to teach something that I loved, to someone who wanted what I had, a wonderful life in a beautiful atmosphere with spectacular scenery. With cars, I was selling a tool that people needed to survive. I preferred teaching, but like anything I got involved with, I did the best I could with what I had to deal with. I was good at selling cars, but living in a resort area with snow on the ground five months out of the year, the Saabs and Toyotas basically sold themselves. Saabs had front wheel drive and Toyotas were Toyotas. Need I say more?

Towards the end of my short career as a car salesman, a woman came into the dealership from Vail one Saturday afternoon. It was my turn to take the next customer. She wanted to buy a Saab. Saabs were more expensive and had a larger margin. I was in a position to make a good commission. She came in, decided on the car she wanted and had all the answers. She was a furrier from Bridge Street (the Rodeo Drive of Vail), with credit cards and a fur coat. She looked and acted extremely wealthy. I turned her over to our sales manager, who finalized the transaction.

On Monday morning at about 7:30 a.m. I received a call from Dick, the owner of the dealership, asking me to stop at the Glenwood Springs police department. The woman had evidently stolen from two or three stores in Vail and a car dealership in Denver, before coming to our dealership. She was finally caught in San Diego on Sunday night, driving the Saab she allegedly purchased from us. The sales manager blamed me for the incident and Dick

Hunting puma with Cheryl Ladd, Rifle, Colorado.

felt he had to let me go. I'd never been fired from a job before and wasn't about to leave on those terms. I spoke up and told him that I didn't think I could work there under these circumstances any longer. Then I got up and left. Dick called me the next day thanking me for my hard work and my honesty and said he would write a nice letter of recommendation. When the word got out, the other three dealerships in Glenwood offered me a job, but I was ready to move on.

Kiki had some problems with a couple of pregnancies. She had a miscarriage at five months with our first pregnancy and got pregnant again several months later, only to have it result in a tubal pregnancy. We were both upset and disappointed with the loss of both attempts to have children. Our marriage began to suffer shortly after. Times were difficult for us financially. I was floating between different jobs trying to find some solid ground to build a financial future for us and it wasn't going very well.

It was always difficult for Sandy, Willie and me to explain that we were Waltners and not Maytags, especially when my younger half-sister and brother were driving exotic cars and flying fancy airplanes. Most people thought that all of us had a secure financial upbringing, when the truth was prior to marrying into the Maytag family, Mom had been a single mother struggling to raise three kids. The easiest way for me to explain it was to say I was brought up in a rags-to-riches, back-to-rags lifestyle. I think when Kiki finally understood we weren't all Maytags, it was time for her to move on. All I could do was the best I knew how. So as much as it upset me, I had to be okay with it and go on with my life.

With the real estate market the way it was, I was lucky enough to sell the little ranch, buy a small house in downtown Carbondale and give Kiki some money. I needed to look for something else to do for work. Julie, a close friend who I had taught skiing with in Snowmass, had become a successful businesswoman. She owned a popular consignment store in Aspen called Cheap Shots, along with an empty building in downtown Carbondale that had previously been the old Kenny's Pharmacy building. She and her husband Barney wanted to open a restaurant in the empty space, but Barney was busy working as John Denver's road manager. Julie's plate was full with Cheap Shots and other deals she was involved with, not to mention raising a family.

She made me a deal I couldn't refuse. After all, I had plenty of experience in the food business consisting of a broken down catering truck and drive-up sandwich shop. I proceeded to find a couple of friends as naive as I was and the Dusty Rose Bar and Restaurant was underway!

Raw oil shale ready to process. Circa 1981.

Oil shale accessory tray   *Finished oil shale*

Dusty Rose Restaurant and Bar
Winter 1981-1982

One of the recruitments, Roy Grice, and I started construction in the fall of 1981. We bought the old bar from the Public House in Aspen (aka The Pub) and purchased tables from the owners of Galena Street East. We bought a few fixtures and some equipment from a Chinese restaurant called the House of Lum, which had moved to Basalt from Aspen in the late seventies. There was no turning back now. Roy and his wife Barbara had some friends who operated a Mexican restaurant in Crested Butte. We brought Alfredo and his wife Neidia on board to operate the kitchen. We opened the doors on the first of June in 1981, and got our liquor license shortly afterward.

At the time Carbondale needed another restaurant. The town was booming with coal, which was back in demand worldwide. Snowmass Coke and Coal and the Mid-Continent Mine were operating at full capacity. Subdivisions were springing up everywhere to house all the miners. The town had come into its own and wasn't just a bedroom community for Aspen. Chris and Teri Chacos, owners of the Village Smithy, a breakfast and lunch eatery, had an extremely successful business. Richard Rider and his wife had a steakhouse across the street from our restaurant, only open for dinner. It seemed fitting to have a lunch and dinner establishment to round out the dining experience in Carbondale.

Unfortunately, the boom didn't last forever. The demand for coal was slowing down in Carbondale. The need was still there worldwide, but other mines newer and more efficient were supplying that demand. Carbondale, no longer a potato Mecca either, reverted back to a small ranching town and bedroom community for Aspen.

Neither Roy nor I wanted to battle with the restaurant any longer. Sixteen-hour days seven days a week — sometimes without a paycheck — got old and tiresome. We sold the Dusty Rose to Skip Bell, who in turn renamed it the Pour House.

Back to Skiing
Winter 1982-1983

A year before selling the restaurant, I had gone back to teaching skiing because I could see that it wasn't going to last. As much as I liked the restaurant business, I was best suited as a ski instructor. Curt Chase, the director of the ski school when I was hired in 1970, had retired. Jon Johanssen, who was my supervisor at Snowmass in the early 70s, was now the ski school director.

Jon and I were at the golf course in Aspen when he asked me if I wanted to come back and teach for him. I literally jumped at the opportunity. He told me I would have to go back through the hiring clinic and jump through a few hoops, but he would try to make it as painless as possible.

Kinda full circle, but glad to be back in my element. 1983

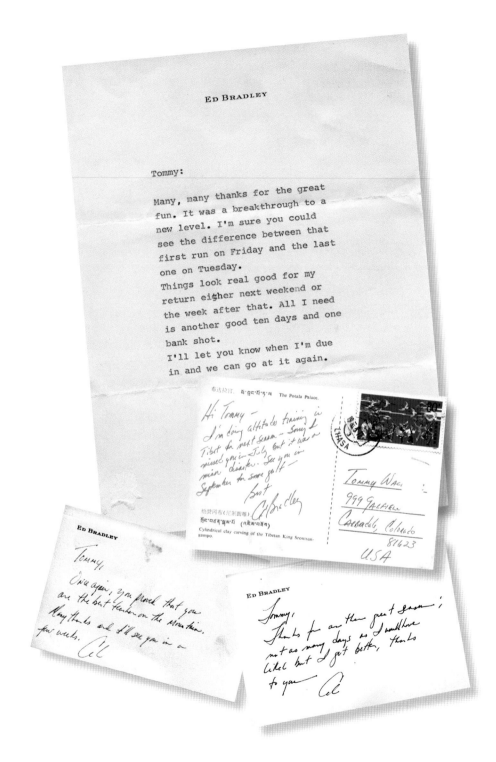

ED BRADLEY

Tommy:

Many, many thanks for the great
fun. It was a breakthrough to a
new level. I'm sure you could
see the difference between that
first run on Friday and the last
one on Tuesday.
Things look real good for my
return either next weekend or
the week after that. All I need
is another good ten days and one
bank shot.
I'll let you know when I'm due
in and we can go at it again.

布达拉宫. ནང་ང་ང་ང་ The Potala Palace.

Hi Tommy —
I'm doing altitude training in
Tibet for next season — sorry I
missed you in July but it was a
minor disaster. See you in
September for some golf —
Best
Ed Bradley

桧赞丙布（足凯圆雕）
ང་ང་ང་ང་ (ང་ང་ང་ང)
Cylindrical clay carving of the Tibetan King Srontsan-
gampo.

Tommy Wac.
999 Galfield
Carbondale, Colorado
81623
USA

ED BRADLEY

Tommy,
Once again, you proved that you
are the best teacher on the mountain.
Many thanks and I'll see you in a
few weeks. Ed

ED BRADLEY

Tommy,
Thanks for another great season;
not as many days as I would have
liked but I got better, thanks
to you. Ed

102

Ed Bradley
Winter 1983-1984

I worked teaching and tending bar at the restaurant that year. In the spring of 1984, Tim Mooney approached me in the Aspen Ski Mart, a local ski shop my close friend Wheels owned, and asked if I would ski with one of his clients who he had skied with once the previous year. In addition to teaching skiing, "Mooney" as we called him, had been working with Jimmy Buffet as a part-time road manager. Mooney was going to take Barney's job as John Denver's road manager, as Barney wanted to pursue the art world as a gallery owner.

I told Mooney I would be more than happy to ski with his client. I asked him where I should meet him and Mooney told me to be at the Ski Mart the next morning at 10:00 a.m. The client's name was Ed Bradley.

It was a beautiful Colorado blue-sky day in March. Whenever I met someone new to ski with I made it a point to arrive a little early, as I didn't do well when I was in a hurry. I arrived at the Ski Mart about 9:40 a.m., walked to the counter and asked Wheels if he had seen this Ed Bradley guy. Right next to me this large black man says, "I'm Ed Bradley." I looked up at him trying not to let him know that he had startled me and introduced myself. He wanted a cup of coffee and a muffin, so I sent him over to the Aspen Square. His girlfriend Cilla was due to arrive in about fifteen minutes to pick us up and take us to Buttermilk. It was Ed's first day that season.

When he left to get his coffee, I asked Wheels, "Who is this guy?" Wheels told me he was the black guy on "60 Minutes." "I can see he is black! What's 60 minutes?" I asked. He proceeded to tell me and I've never missed an episode since.

Cilla showed up in a Jeep Eagle four-wheel-drive Wagoneer, we loaded up our equipment and off to Buttermilk we went! Well we didn't get more than a couple of blocks when Ed turned around in the passenger seat held up a "joint" and said, "Do you mind?" I responded, "Not if I can partake!"

We arrived at Buttermilk, put our gear on and headed up the lift. He told me that he had only skied a few times. Last year he skied once with Mooney and Jack Nicholson came along with a couple of his buddies. They all referred to themselves as "The Thundering Herd". We got off the lift and headed towards West Buttermilk because it was the gentlest slope. I immediately understood "Thundering Herd". He looked like a runaway hayride! I took off, caught up with him slowed him down and started our lesson. I have to admit Cilla and I were laughing pretty hard, but I was uncertain if it was solely the result of the joint.

We had a great day and Ed continued to improve. He was very athletic. He had played a lot of sports in high school and worked out religiously in the gym. As the day went on he kept asking me if he could "cut one loose?" I didn't know exactly what he meant. All I did know was that I didn't want this "runaway hayride" to hurt himself. At the end of the day he asked me again if he could "cut one loose"; I looked at Cilla a little dumbfounded and said, "Suit yourself." Well, he took off like a bat out of hell! I looked at Cilla and said, "I thought he had to fart and I didn't want him to have to hold it any longer." We were both laughing so hard we could barely ski down to him.

At the end of the day, as we headed back to the car, he told me that he would be in town for two more days and asked if we could ski together again. Having as much fun as we had, there was no way I was going to miss another day with either of them.

We skied once more at Buttermilk, then graduated to Aspen Mountain for his last day. He had a lot of fun and wanted to try to come out a few more times before we closed for the season, so we exchanged phone numbers and addresses. We would stay in touch, and if he couldn't reach me at home, he would contact the Ski Mart or ski school to find me.

The day before I was to start with Ed again, I was teaching another student on Aspen Mountain when all of a sudden my name showed up on a blackboard at the Little Nell Chair. It read: "Tom Waltner please contact ski patrol immediately." By the time I got to a phone, I had ridden three lifts, all with my name on a blackboard. I went into the patrol shack on the top of the mountain. By this time I was getting a little concerned. The patrol gave me a phone number and a phone to use, and I called the number. It was Ed letting me know he had arrived and would see me at the Ski Mart in the morning. As I was walking out of the patrol shack, the patrol asked me if everything was okay? "Oh yeah things are fine," I said, but in the back of my mind I was thinking, "This is going to be one twisted relationship — and I could hardly wait!"

Sold Dusty Rose
Summer 1984

I worked at the restaurant, tending bar two or three nights a week. Things were rather slow in Carbondale, except for the usual summer events including the Fourth of July, Mountain Fair and Potato Days to round out the summer.

Now that the mining had come to an end, leaving many without work, things seemed to be more depressing. Alcohol and drug use were on the rise. Being in the bar business wasn't all bad, but it could get rough more times than not, with fights breaking out for all sorts of reasons, relationships ending, money, work, you name it.

Every evening about 11:00 p.m. or so the local police would make their nightly rounds to all the late night establishments. They were welcome by all of us in the business. It was fairly easy to tell which patrons were using drugs by looking at them and trying to understand what they were saying.

I'd come in to clean in the morning after working the previous night, to get the place ready to open for lunch. I'd find matchbooks among other things on the floor. I'd keep the ones with the Dusty Rose logo on them and throw them back in the basket with the others. I immediately noticed bindles of cocaine in the back of the matchbooks. Since I didn't like cocaine very much, especially at nine in the morning, I'd throw it away.

After a few times, I figured out that when the cops came in to make their rounds the people with drugs would panic and throw them on the floor along with the matchbooks, and leave. Well when the police left, I would come out from behind the bar and pick up any matchbooks on the floor to see if they had drugs in them. I would know who it belonged to and sell it back to them the next night. I usually started my next night shift with a $30.00 or $40.00 head start on my tips. In October, we finalized the paperwork with Skip. Roy and I were glad to be out of the restaurant business.

Even the horses were served during Carbondale's Coal Bust.

Who's that behind those Revos?

Ed and Mont Tremblant
Winter 1984-1985

I was so glad to be back teaching skiing again, knowing this was my calling. I didn't have to think about work as far as winters were concerned. I still needed to figure out what to do in the summers, but something would always come up and I didn't think that would change. I would be resourceful enough to find something to do.

Ed came at Thanksgiving and was like a little kid who had just discovered a new love. He came again the week leading up to Christmas day and would leave to spend the holidays with his mom in Philadelphia. He came out a few more times and bought a condo in town just east of Main Street and Original Curve. Every time Ed came, I would get so excited. He always had great stories to share.

After about twenty days of skiing that year, I saw a noticeable improvement in Ed. Good enough that he told me the story of when he first skied with some of his college friends in Canada at Mont Tremblant. Like a lot of "friends" do, they take you up to the top of the bunny slope, show you around a little bit, then basically cut you loose so that you're on your own. Ed got to the top of the bunny hill and fell off the lift. His buddies put him back together and showed him a snowplow and how to get back up when he fell, knowing he was going to fall.

Well, Ed took off from the top blindly determined not to fall. As he started to tell me this story I thought about that runaway hayride. He passed the lift at the bottom of the hill where he had started, zoomed by the Base Lodge where he had purchased his lift ticket, into the parking lot where he had parked and down the road that led to the ski area. He finally sat down at the first big switchback in the road, after coming out of both skis, losing his poles and sliding on his butt to the top of a snow bank in the middle of the switchback. He gathered up all his gear, threw his skis over his shoulder (the only thing he could do half-right) and walked back up through the parking lot to the Base Lodge — right into the bar.

At this point, I laughed so hard and thought to myself, "Now he is all mine!" I was so grateful to Mooney for hooking Ed and me up because I knew this was going to be a life-long relationship. Ed loved skiing; he bought a house in Aspen and we got along great!

Dental Assistant
Summer 1985

Back in November, just prior to the start of ski season, I had my teeth cleaned. Not going to the dentist regularly, the hygienist spent a lot of time cleaning the inside lower back of my front teeth, to the point that her fingers were cramping up from de-scaling and removing the stain from cigarettes and coffee. She told me that this wasn't uncommon, but since I had only seen the dentist once every couple of years, mine were particularly in need of a thorough cleaning. I left the dentist's office feeling a bit sorry for this cute little hygienist, thinking there had to be a better way.

I had a bad dentist growing up who would offer us candy suckers for being good little patients when we left the office. Just prior to moving to Aspen, I had to have all the work redone including 14 inlays. My new dentist told me that in my case brushing wasn't necessarily the solution; flossing would be extremely beneficial as my teeth were so close together.

By the time I got home, I had in my mind invented the perfect toothbrush. It was a two-headed brush with dental floss in the handle. This way if you weren't flossing regularly it was your own fault because in order to brush your teeth you had to hold the dental floss in your hand. One end was the same as a regular toothbrush, while the other end had the bristles at an angle designed to clean the inside back of your lower teeth. I called it the "Dental Assistant".

I immediately made a rough prototype and took it to my friend Alfonse, an engineer who worked behind my old restaurant. He loved the concept and did a precise drawing for a friend of his in California who specialized in injection type molding. I took my prototype and a copy of the drawing to Denver to meet with a patent attorney, who performed a patent search. By the time summer had come to an end, the patent attorney sent me a letter with the results of the search. I was amazed to find out how many other people manufacturers and companies had thought of the same thing even as far back as the early 1900s. All of the previous patents had expired a long time ago. I had never seen anything like it on the market. The attorney told me that I could apply for a design patent, but Alfonse suggested I hold off until we could find out a little more about manufacturing the product.

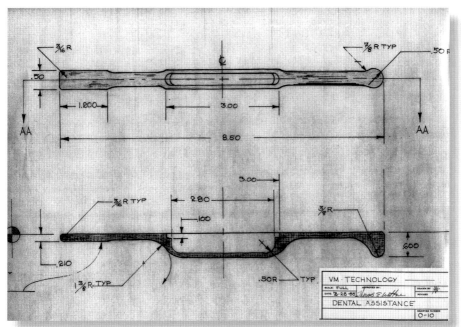

Manufacturing design including a detail for Dental Assistant

New Clients
Winter 1985-1986

Alfonse traveled back and forth to California and had his friend make an injection mold for several prototypes, similar to what we would make for production. Meanwhile, I continued teaching skiing that winter. Ed and I skied about 30 days. Between Ed's trips I'd ski with new clients from the private lesson desk or from other pros who had double bookings. It worked out great being able to help each other out with work. Ajax was the most challenging mountain in Aspen, so it didn't get much walk-in traffic for ski lessons. Most people who skied there were already experienced. I was fortunate enough to pick up a couple of new clients. One skier, who was given to me by another pro, was Irving Azoff. Irving and I hit it off really well. He was big in the music industry and came to Aspen a lot. He managed Jimmy Buffett and the Eagles when they were all just starting their music careers.

I also picked up a couple from Atlanta, Georgia, John and Judy Riddle. John played baseball for the Atlanta Braves minor league team and Judy was an airline stewardess for Delta. John was involved in a lot of different businesses. He had a retail store in Atlanta and did special service awards for companies in the southeast including Coca-Cola, Southern Bell and a couple of energy companies.

He bid and got the contract for Coca-Cola's 100-anniversary parade. He was going to set up all the seating for a four-mile stretch through the streets of downtown Atlanta and asked me to come out and help. I thought it would be a great opportunity, especially since I had never been east of Denver other than the trip to Lake Placid for the Winter Olympics in 1980.

Coca-Cola and the Dental Assistant
Summer 1986

As summer approached, Alfonse and I got together to evaluate the Dental Assistant Toothbrush and decided that I should travel to downtown LA to discuss the possibility of starting production on the product. First I went to Atlanta to help John with the Coca-Cola anniversary. The job was to take about three weeks. I worked with one of John's partners to put up the bleacher type seats along the four-mile parade route through downtown

Atlanta. It was quite impressive the way John orchestrated the project. Everything went relatively smoothly and I was home by early June.

Shortly after, I jumped in my car and drove to LA to meet with Alfonse, who by this time, had the molding for the handle ready for manufacturing. I went downtown to talk to the only person in the United States who had the machinery to put bristles in brushes. I soon found out that the U.K. was where most brushes with bristles were manufactured.

The manufacturer loved the concept, but explained to me that it was impossible to do it the way Alfonse and I had thought. The machinery wasn't capable of putting bristles in the brushes with the required angle to make the brush work the way it needed to in order to clean the inside back of the lower teeth. He did say it would be possible if we manufactured the handle in two separate pieces and put them together in some sort of snap capacity. Unfortunately, by doing it that way we would run into liability problems. If the angle piece broke off in use the brush handle could cut the gums pretty severely.

So it was back to the drawing board. I was learning more and more about product development by the manufacturer. He told me an interesting story about a guy who had come to him with a product he had developed and patented. It was a toothbrush with a two-colored handle like a candy cane. The injection mold process was made in two pieces with two different colors that snapped together. They were made in red and white, green and white, and various other colors with the bristles placed inside. The guy had a friend who was a district sales manager for the Safeway Corporation grocery chain. The manager for Safeway ordered several dozen of the multi-colored toothbrushes and put them in a dozen or so grocery stores in his territory as a test market. Kids and parents alike loved the brushes; they were the first toothbrushes to sell out in all the Safeway stores where they'd been stocked.

Safeway expanded to several other stores in southern California and the inventor, knowing his product was a winner, bought his wife a Mercedes and started an addition on his house. Things were going really well for this guy and Safeway ordered a million or so for all its stores in the U.S. Well the inventor couldn't meet the order and lost the contract. If I planned to continue building up a product development company, hearing that story was beneficial to me. I was definitely going to pursue it, but wasn't going to give up my day job teaching skiing.

Silver Queen Gondola
Winter 1986-1987

Having been under construction the previous two years, the whole base area of Aspen Mountain looked like a war zone. The Little Nell Hotel was being built and the Silver Queen Gondola installed. It was a high-speed lift which would carry six passengers from the bottom to the top of Aspen Mountain in 13 minutes. At least that's the way it was advertised and operated for the first year. It was a ten million dollar project for the lift alone. Marvin Davis and 20th Century Fox, the new owners of the Aspen Ski Company, were making the largest capital investment ever for a ski area in North America. (Interestingly enough, for the 10 years that Marvin Davis owned the Aspen Ski Company he never once rode in the Silver Queen Gondola.)

Two more quad chairs were put in place at the top of the mountain. Along with the five star Little Nell Hotel, all this cost tens of millions of dollars. Not everyone was excited to see all the developments in the former little mining town, but it sure changed the way Aspen Mountain skied. A powder day now lasted only about two hours, and après ski at the bottom of Little Nell went from a huge deck with five bars to a five star hotel that no one wanted to drink in or have anything to do with. Needless to say, après ski bars popped up all over town. At least five opened to replace the ones that had been at the base.

The 13-minute lift ride that had been advertised only lasted one year. When Poma, the lift manufacturer, returned to service the lift at the end of the first season, they explained that if the company wanted to get the life expectancy out of the gondola, they would have to run it more cautiously.

The locals gave the gondola many nicknames that first year. One that stood out was "The Silver Bucket." Rather than hauling silver out of the hills it spanned, it hauled skiers who skied over the old mine dumps it served. To this day people still refer to it as the "Bucket".

That year I skied about thirty more days with Ed, and about twenty with Irving, which worked out great for me. For the most part, I would ski with Irving and his family for two weeks at Christmas and one week during spring break. Ed spent more time with his mom at Christmas, which allowed him to stay away from the bigger crowds that he didn't like. This worked out better for both of us because he could spread out his time in Aspen and be with his mom.

It was a great release for Ed from his work schedule to be able to come and go between stories he would shoot for 60 Minutes. He also scheduled speaking engagements at colleges, large company gatherings and just about anywhere people were interested in hearing him talk about his life. I was always fascinated by what he had to say. When Ed came to town to ski, he was like a breath of fresh air. He always had something new and interesting to talk about. At some point, I asked him how he got started in journalism. Over our twenty some years of skiing together, I got to hear it all.

Ed grew up poor in Philadelphia. His father had a vending machine company and as Ed would say, his dad always had a chunk of pocket change. Ed attended college on a football scholarship and became a schoolteacher. He traveled to the south of France one summer and, falling in love with it, decided to stay. He got a job working with a producer who did documentary film work for CBS. When his boss got an assignment he didn't want to take, he would pass it on to Ed. An assignment to film a group of blind kids at the Louvre Museum in Paris came up, and the producer passed it on to Ed. Ed produced and directed the documentary featuring the kids climbing all over the statues at the Louvre and explaining how they felt about living with their disability. As it turned out, the well-received documentary won a couple of awards.

CBS offered Ed a position in New York. He was given a good job with his own office, but Ed didn't like being trapped inside. One day, he walked into his boss's office and told him that he didn't like being confined inside and wondered if there was something else he could do outside on location; anything to keep him out of an office. Ed looked at his producer and said, "I'd rather be in Vietnam!"

The producer looked at Ed and said, "Seriously?" Ed left for Vietnam shortly after. I looked up at Ed and said, "So the rest is history?" Ed said, "That's pretty much how it happened." As we continued to spend more one-on-one time together, I really began to feel as though I was a part of his life.

Ed and me 1987

Ed, Cilla and friend. Aspen Mountain 1989.

Danny Wardwell, Don "the Duke" Dixon, Ed and I enjoying the ride together.

Back Surgery and the Backpack
Summer 1987

I've had a bad back for a long time, going back to my high school days. It seems as though all of the wear and tear my body had sustained over the course of my life, was due to activities involving tremendous impact on my back. While skiing with Irving during Christmas the past year, I was clipped by a guest near the top of Aspen Mountain and knocked over. It may have been the straw that broke the "Tommy's" back. I dealt with it all winter and needed to do lots of stretching, taking copious amounts of Advil. My doctor told me that when chiropractors were no longer able to help I might want to explore surgery or change my lifestyle. The latter wasn't an option. At 37, I felt as though I was just getting started.

Dr. Kirk scheduled a laminectomy surgery for me in the Spring of 1987 in Aspen. The surgery went fine. Other than the pain of the drain in the middle of my back and the sciatica, I was feeling pretty good. I was released from the hospital five days later and spent the rest of the time recuperating at home. I soon became bored. Reading wasn't an option for me as I still wasn't very good at it, especially with all my daydreaming and lack of concentration. The only thing I was interested in was product development.

I started reminiscing about my high school days, and my friend Craig's father who was an inventor, and about my toothbrush design that I was still passionate about. Sadly, it was out of the question. It occurred to me that I could create a bag with two applications, a backpack option, or a shoulder-strap option, making it look just like the Silver Queen Gondola buckets (cars). I designed it and had a seamstress friend of mine in

Gondola backpack/shoulder bag

Carbondale make them for me, with the intention of selling them in Aspen. She started with six dozen, which I sold to Carl's Pharmacy, Aspen Drug and a couple of hiking and camping stores. This continued for a couple of years, until the gondola became just another ski lift and interest faded.

Rosie O'Grady's Flying Circus
Winter 1987-1988

I skied with Ed at Thanksgiving and whenever he could come. I skied with Irving at Christmas and spring break. Between the time I spent skiing with Ed or Irving, I picked up some other clients George McKerrow from Atlanta and Bob Snow from Orlando. Both became very close friends, who I admired tremendously and felt fortunate to have as clients. George came out a couple of times a year and I got to know him really well. He was a successful restaurant operator who began as a district manager for a chain of steak houses in Texas called Victoria Station. He later started his own chain of steak houses in Atlanta called Long Horn Steaks. George and I were the same age and had similar interests including golf, girls and fun. We hit it off great!

Bob Snow was the founder of Church Street Station, a theme park in downtown Orlando. Unlike Disney World, or other places in Orlando with amusement park themes, it consisted of a neighborhood of restaurants, entertainment, live shows, street activities and arcades. Bob's partner, Joe Kittinger, ran a division of the station called "Rosie O'Grady's Flying

Bob taking me for a ride. No tricks right? Wrong! Circa 1987

Circus". Joe handled anything and everything off the ground including: ballooning, sky-writing airplanes that pulled advertising banners, and sky-diving aerobatics. If it happened in the air, it was Joe's department.

Bob and I skied together frequently, occasionally with his wife Linda and son Christopher, as well as Joe and his wife Sherry. The first time he brought Joe out with him, Bob advised me that Joe would be my new project. He went on to tell me that if I decided to take him on it wouldn't be very difficult, as Joe was used to jumping out of weather balloons from 102,800 feet. He had set records for speed and free fall distances in 1960, all for the sake of testing aerospace suits for NASA. Bob didn't think a little ski hill would scare him. Over the years, I got to know Joe and Sherry quite well. His list of accomplishments never ceased to amaze me.

Joe and Sherry being honored for his contribution to American Aviation, a park dedicated in Joe's name.

Sherry, Joanie, me, Joe, Bob and Christopher (Bob & Linda's son) and Linda enjoying dinner in Basalt.
Circa 1994.

Golf
Summer 1988

I hadn't been to Baja for a while, so I felt a trip to visit my close friends Mike and Deirdre was due. Tony Rutgers, a co-worker and longtime friend of Mike's and mine, boarded the Warner Brothers jet with Irving. Then we went to California for a little fishing time with friends and to thaw out from the winter.

Tony and I flew with Mike to Laredo, about a hundred miles south of Mulege, on the Baja Peninsula. We looked at a house Mike was interested in purchasing from a farming acquaintance in Brawley, California and spent five days camping and fishing. We always ate well on those trips, catching fresh fish and diving for clams. Raised in Fiji, Tony was a great cook, especially when it came to seafood.

We left Laredo and flew Tony to Cabo, where he met his wife, and stayed for a week before returning to Aspen. I left Brawley for Santa Monica to stay with my high school friend and roommate from Aspen in the early 70s. It was my 30-year Pali High School reunion. The party was at the "Beach Club" on the Pacific Coast Highway at the mouth of Santa Monica Canyon, my high school stomping grounds.

When I returned home, I played a lot of golf. Golf was a great way to entertain potential real estate clients. With golf courses starting to pop up everywhere, the real estate market was slowly starting to climb out of the slump it had been in. I did have a few real estate closings that year, just enough to keep me in the loop.

I played in a couple of golf tournaments that year. One was in Atlanta with George, the annual Longhorn Steak tournament, benefiting the Scottish Rite Children's Hospital in Atlanta. The other was the High Country Shoot Out Golf Tournament put on by Jimmy Buffett and Ed Podolak, an Aspen resident and pro football veteran with the Kansas City Chiefs. Ed Bradley played in that tournament and asked his friend Hunter Thompson join him. They were always a colorful duo. Ed and Hunter had become good friends when they both worked as journalists for the Democratic National Convention throughout the 80s.

I will never forget the incident on the driving range prior to the shotgun start of the tournament. Hunter was determined to get a birdie, so he pulled a shotgun out of his golf bag and fired it. Ed and I about fell over. Hunter got in trouble, but was able to convince the authorities it was all in good fun, so the tournament went on.

Golfing with George. Atlanta 1987

Ed and Irving
Winter 1988-1989

My ski career was beginning to take off like clockwork. Ed would come for Thanksgiving and periodically throughout the season. Unlike most clients I skied with year after year, Ed brought new stories and adventures with him. I always looked forward to skiing with Ed. Irving on the other hand, was a troublemaker, so I always had to ski with my guard up. There was never a dull moment when Irving was around. I'd come out from lunch to find my skis missing or my uniform gone; it was always something. It finally got to the point that if I let it bother me, he would feed off my misery and continue with his pranks.

One morning I got a call from Irving telling me that it had snowed about a foot overnight. He decided he wanted to ski Tiehack because Aspen Mountain would get skied off quickly with all the high speed lifts. We went to Tiehack and there wasn't a soul there, allowing us to ski untracked snow for most of the morning. The patrol had closed off Racer's Edge, Tiehack Parkway, and Javelin, the steepest runs on Tiehack.

At about 11:30 a.m., Irving and I were riding up the lift and noticed the patrol opening up the closed areas. Irving looked over at me and said, "Okay here's what we're going to do!" I told him not to get me in trouble while I was in uniform. He proceeded to tell me that he'd ski down to where the patrol had opened everything and re-close it, allowing us to ski it the rest of the day all to ourselves. Well it worked! Irving and I skied until we got tired and then Irving feeling proud of himself, re-opened it for the public on our last run at about 1:00 p.m.

LA Dodgers and Cush 'N' Carry
Summer 1989

Irving owned a record company and was not only involved in managing musicians, but ran all of the merchandising at the California concerts and sports venues. He offered me a job that summer to work for the LA Dodgers, handling program sales outside Dodger's Stadium before the games started. At the end of the second inning, after most of the fans had arrived, I would go inside and help the vendors sell souvenirs inside the stadium.

Standing outside of the stadium selling programs was wild. The fans showed up with kids and binoculars, so they could get an extra close view of whatever was going to happen over the next two plus hours. They tried to fish two bucks out of a pocket for a program, while juggling all of their stuff. Inside, when the seventh inning stretch would start the fans — including all the pretty Hollywood starlets — would come to the souvenir stands to purchase a seat cushion. After seven innings of baseball, the seats would start to get hard and uncomfortable.

Suddenly, I was inspired. Thinking about a bag that could open into a seat cushion, I designed a prototype on a napkin in the clubhouse. I sat with one of the manufacturers of the Dodger warm-up jackets that we sold in the souvenir stands. He took my idea to his seamstresses and they made a working prototype of my first "Cush N' Carry", an activity bag and seat cushion combined.

When I got home, I immediately went to Denver and met with Kyle Rost, a patent attorney, who applied for a design patent. We were granted that patent in 1993 and it wouldn't expire for 13 years. I found a company in Taiwan, "Shining Gold" a manufacturer that immediately tried to market the concept themselves, attempting to sell them in the U.S. Thankfully, Kyle was able to stop any product they tried to get into America.

I found a manufacturer in the clothing district in downtown LA willing to manufacture them for a couple of years. I sold them as a promotional give-away at golf tournaments, volleyball tournaments and a few retail outlets. Later, a company owner who had gotten one at a golf tournament approached me with a contract to manufacture and market the product paying me a royalty. It made sense to me to accept the terms of our agreement, as they had all the licensing rights for pro, college, high school, and any other sports related events, including the Olympics and Nascar.

Cush 'N' Carry goes large, Nascar 1998.

Denver Merchandising Mart

NEW PRODUCT

CUSH 'N CARRY
Activity Bag / Seat Cushions

The Cush 'N Carry Activity Bag is great for carrying all necessities for sports events, concerts, picnics, etc. It works as a student's book bag or a mother's baby bag.

If the side and bottom are unzipped, it serves as a seat and back cushion for chairs.

The bag also totally separates into two individual seat cushions.

For information and comments contact:

The Cush 'N Carry Activity Bag is warranted against manufacturing defects.

Cush 'N' Carry point of purchase flyer.

125

Sailing and Golf
1989-1990

I always felt I was in my element when ski season rolled around. I was extremely comfortable on snow. When I was skiing, no matter who it was with, I was confident. I could have been with a movie star, CEO of a major corporation, doctors, lawyers or developers. It didn't make any difference because they needed me. They had to let me be in charge if they were to enjoy their ski vacation.

There were times I felt as though I was a taxicab driver. Clients would consistently ask me where were the best restaurants, places to stay, nightclubs and drugs. It didn't make much difference what they wanted, they felt at ease asking a ski instructor. We were the celebrities in Aspen. They had come to ski, just wanting to get away from their work and play for a while, where hopefully no one would care or even notice them.

At this point, all of my clients were very close friends, who found Aspen to be a year-round playground. Most of them either had second homes in Aspen or were looking for one. They would come as often as possible to ski in the winter, hike, bike, fish, play tennis or golf. Except for the ocean, Aspen had it all.

However, sailing was very popular. Even I had a small Hobie Cat and loved sailing. Ruedi Reservoir above Basalt was a very popular spot for water skiing, fishing, sailing and camping. I purchased a building site at Ruedi as an investment so I could enjoy the lake — a perfect spot to leave my sailboat. There was also a yacht club at the lake, where I was a member for a few years. Most people didn't realize that the top of Independence Pass and the top of the Frying Pan River Valley above Ruedi Reservoir were a stone's throw apart. If the Frying Pan road could have gone several miles further it would have met Highway 82, just on the Leadville side of Independence Pass.

I spent a lot of time in Atlanta with George watching his chain of restaurants grow. Not only did he have seven or eight steak houses, but

Joanie giving Cush 'N' Carry to participants of Longhorns Steak Golf Classic, 1990.

also had a fish and ribs concept called "Skeeters" and a roadhouse barbecue called "Wyolene's". In 1992, I sold George about 100 Cush N' Carry bags for a golf tournament. My girlfriend Joanie and I went to promote my product and of course play a little golf. The bag was very well received and I wrote a couple of orders for a few dozen more. I did the same that year for the Buffet/Podolak "High Country Shoot Out" golf tournament in Aspen. People really seemed to like getting something other than a T-shirt or hat at events.

Meanwhile, Bob Snow had sold Church Street Station to the Chinese and was interested in pursuing a gaming theme park. I spent some time with Bob traveling around Colorado for the possibility of doing something in Black Hawk or Central City, just outside of Denver. These old mining towns had just been approved for gambling and Bob thought that getting in early might be to his benefit. We researched the possibility, but decided his plan was best suited for Las Vegas. His vision was to bring back a Wild West theme. Developing a portion of downtown Las Vegas would be a better venue. Las Vegas, of course, had all the resources and the Strip was more in tune to golf and nightclub shows. He thought downtown would welcome a different and more western theme. His partner Joe would handle the Rosie O'Grady's Flying Circus portion of the theme park without interfering with the airport airspace, as downtown was a little further from the Las Vegas airport than the Strip. The education I received from my ski clients like Bob and George was invaluable. I felt so lucky to be a part of it and to see what they had to go through to make their dreams a reality.

Sailing at Ruedi. Circa 1990.

Earthquake 1991

I had been working on a board game since 1990, but could never really figure out just how to do it. I had a name for it, but that was about it. It all started with a trip I had made to LA when looking for a manufacturer for Cush 'N' Carry. I was staying with some friends in the San Fernando Valley when I was woken up to pictures falling on the floor and things falling out of cabinets. I had never felt an earthquake before, although people had told me stories. This was the real deal.

When I got back to Carbondale I just missed an earthquake that had happened close to Mt. Sopris, just south of Carbondale, that had been felt in town. As I was reading about it in the paper, it struck me how to design the game.

It was a pretty simple concept and it came together fairly fast. The concept was similar to that of building card houses when we were kids. Rather than cards, I called them building walls. There were four kinds of walls: brick, wood siding, stucco and metal siding. Each player received a stack of cards with their respective wall type. Each wall had a number from 1 through 9 on one side. A player would shuffle their stack of walls and play from the top of the stack. The board had a built-in timer. Once it was set, no one would know when it would go off … and POOF! The board would shake and all the walls would come down. There was a 6-sided die with the numbers 2, 3, and 4, with each number having two faces. The game began by deciding who would start and then throwing the dice to determine the number of walls to put up. The timer would go off, the board would shake, the walls would fall and a scoring system would determine the winner.

I contacted a couple of board game companies including Milton Bradley. I was put in touch with a company who evaluated products and developed them. A lot is involved with having a concept protected and gaining copyright. I had learned through experience not to chase nickels with dollars. You can spend a lot of time and money before you find out it's not feasible. In my case, I was about five years too late with all the technology and electronics already in the marketplace. Companies were looking for toys and games with a little more sophistication and high tech.

Cool-Apse
1993

Joanie and I used to vacation in Puerto Escondido, a small fishing village in southern Mexico in Oaxaca. Just a half-hour flight from Puerto Escondido was the ancient Zapotec capital and archaeological site of the Monte Alban ruins, a fifteenth century pre-Columbian city with beautiful architecture. It was a very popular beach resort for Europeans, Canadians and the upper class Mexican population. I liked it for its jungle beauty, where several Tarzan movies were filmed. The waves, a beach break that surfed just like the Bonsai Pipeline in Hawaii, was also the big attraction for me. Sometimes the surf got so big — I was too scared to go in it.

Like all of Mexico, refrigeration was a problem and ice was hard to come by. Every time Joanie and I went there I would tell her how great it would be to have a cooler in our room for beer and water, but coolers were cumbersome to travel with. One afternoon on the beach, after we had finished packing to leave the next day, I took a piece of cardboard and made a prototype of a cooler that folded up to about the size of a game board. When we got home I took the prototype to the seamstress who had made my gondola backpacks. We made a working prototype of what I called "Cool-Apse."

I took it down to Denver to see if Kyle felt we could patent it. He liked the concept and thought we could possibly get a utility patent because of the way the lid of the cooler worked. It was designed to force all the outside air out of the cooler, rather than trapping it inside and keep the cold air in when the lid was removed and then replaced.

Once again, rather than pay the expense to go ahead with the patent, I talked to the R&D department of Coleman and Igloo and asked them to take a look and tell me what they thought. Knowing they could steal the idea, because large corporations seldom sign any type of disclosure agreement, I decided to take a chance. When dealing with people, honesty and integrity go a long way (i.e. dealing with people in corporate America CEOs and business owners, etc.). This was something I learned teaching skiing. They were very honest with me and liked my idea, but soft coolers had been introduced and they felt "Cool-Apse" was a little late coming to the market. I looked at it as another learning experience and was thankful I didn't spend a lot of money on a product that wasn't suited for the market.

Cool-Apse for travel!

Cool-Apse on the go!

Ruedi House
1994

For the past couple of years the Carbondale population had been on the rise. It had really become a bedroom community for Aspen, where the rent had forced hundreds of employees to look elsewhere to live and raise their families. Adding to that, the workforce had become largely Hispanic.

During those days of the Dusty Rose Restaurant, when I moved into town from the ranch, I had bought a small house next to the largest apartment complex in Carbondale. It had been thirty percent occupied. By the mid-90s, capacity had climbed to one hundred percent, consisting of Hispanic transients doing the work in Aspen most locals refused to do anymore. Work like shoveling snow, housekeeping and general grunt labor.

Don't get me wrong. I'd spent a lot of time in Mexico and liked the people, but living a "Big Gulp" away from 7-Eleven across the street from Circle Supers, soon to be City Market, and a stone's throw from Joanie's family, was just becoming too much for us. My lot in Ruedi was starting to lure my thoughts back to building a log home close enough to the lake to see it and enjoy what the mountains had to offer. After all, getting away from city life is what brought me to Aspen in the first place.

My good friend George from Atlanta offered me a construction loan at a better interest rate than I could get at the bank. I don't know if I would have qualified for a loan and private investors were a little more flexible in the event that anything unfavorable should come up. About the time we got the roof on, my contractor Dave, fell off the roof and dislocated his ankle tearing all the surrounding tendons and ligaments.

Before we started the project, we discussed wages, insurance and responsibilities. I was determined to build this house for no more than $75.00 per square foot. That was all I could afford. Dave and I had worked together teaching skiing and I had put his father in touch with my mom to build her log home in Starwood. Being friends, we agreed with a handshake that I would pay him a few more dollars per hour as an independent contractor and he would be covered by his own health insurance policy. He decided to sue me and I learned very quickly the laws involving independent contractors and workman's compensation.

Thank God I wasn't drinking or drugging during this project, but under these circumstances, the temptation may have led most people down that road. I was extremely depressed and Joanie was dealing with her own depression and medical issues. Joanie had a pharmacy background and she made an appointment for me to see a doctor in Glenwood Springs. I liked my own doctor, but Joanie didn't because she had had a previous falling out with him over prescribed medication. So I went to see a doctor she recommended.

The first question she asked me as I sat in her office was, "Why did I think I was depressed?" I responded by telling her, "Because I was sitting in a stranger's office and telling her so." Her response was to give me a worksheet questionnaire with about 30 questions relating to previous history and thoughts of suicide. When she came back into the room, she sat down and looked over the questionnaire. She came to the same conclusion that I had. "You are depressed, alright." She gave me some antidepressants and sent me on my way.

I managed to get through the lawsuit without losing everything, including my life. I had a close friend help me find someone I didn't know to finish my log home. After the work was completed, I sold my house in Carbondale and paid George back for the construction loan. I also quit taking the antidepressants, despite the doctor advising me that to do so without medical supervision would be dangerous. The drugs had made me feel more confused than the depression itself, so I was willing to take that chance. The house took a year and a half to build. With all the problems I had I was still able to build it for less than $100.00 per square foot.

My cabin in the mountains at Ruedi Reservoir. Circa 1994

Joanie and I Get Married
1996

Now that Joanie and I had settled into our new home, I was already looking for a new summer project. My mom had been making mustard for years, giving it away for Christmas gifts and other occasions. When Mom moved away from Aspen, people were always asking me about her mustard. They liked it so much I asked her for the recipe, which she gladly provided me.

The recipe she used was not cost effective for the market, but then again money wasn't an issue for something of limited availability and high demand. So I experimented, made some adjustments to the original recipe, and was able to come up with a product that tasted like Mom's, but cost less to produce. Joanie really liked the mustard, but hated the way it smelled while being made. She thought up the name, "Tommy's Magic Mustard" because it was magically delicious, even though it smelled atrocious during the cooking process.

I teamed up with Dean Logan of Logan Stock Manufacturing. The facility was located in the Mid-Valley Design Center in Basalt. I opened about forty accounts between Aspen and Glenwood and sold several hundred cases of the product over the next couple of years. Since it was very well received in the valley, I had great plans for expanding the line and selling it statewide. Eventually, Dean's facility had to become a F.D.A. approved kitchen because of the products he was processing, so I was out of a place to manufacture my mustard.

Ed Bradley loved the mustard and was willing to help in anyway necessary. I looked into having it processed in Denver, renting my own place and installing a commercial kitchen to accommodate the small co-packing operation. Nothing seemed to work out financially, so I put it on the back burner for a while.

Joanie and I got married that summer and my close and longtime friend Jim from Houston was my best man. Jim came out and spent a couple of weeks. He had a condo in Breckenridge and I went over there to play golf and talk about the "good ole days" in June Lake, Aspen, the oil shale boom and his project with Shell Oil. Shell was buying up old Southland Corporation convenience stores (7-Eleven) with the idea of getting into the convenience store arena. They called their concept ETD, "Experience The Difference" and were expanding at a rapid pace. Jim was put in charge of the convenience store division for Shell Oil.

I had gotten an idea stemming from my bad experience with my friend, who had sued me while building my house. Aspen had gone from "Dogs, Dirt and Dope" in the seventies to "Sex, Drugs and Rock and Roll" in the eighties to "Rich, Rude and the Greedy" in the nineties. Jim and I both felt there just wasn't enough kindness in the world, so together we launched the "World Kindness Campaign" using slogans on bumper stickers, buttons, hats ,T-shirts and product labels. We hoped to use corporations and companies like Shell to help spread the message of kindness worldwide. Jim and I spent a few years working on this, but it was just too big and required too much in order to actually make it happen. Even though we had made progress coming close to turning it into a reality, it required larger resources than were available to us to continue.

Jim and I. Ruedi cabin. Circa 1998,

MiLLENNiUM & BEYOND

2000+

Loops for Lupus
1999

Joanie and I had been struggling for the past six months or so. Her depression worsened. In my view she had made some poor career decisions. Adding to her demise was her need for back surgery and discovering her mother had been diagnosed with Lupus. I knew nothing about Lupus, in fact I had never even heard of it. Joanie needed to see a specialist in Denver for the nerve pain she was suffering from and I thought it would be a good opportunity for me to learn more about Lupus.

I made an appointment to see the executive director for the Colorado Chapter of the Lupus Foundation. She was able to explain to me just exactly what Lupus was and who was at risk for contracting the disease. The number of people who had Lupus was startling. I was overwhelmed to learn that ninety percent of people affected were women. One in two hundred had this disease whether they knew it or not, partly because it was a "non-glamorous disease". People who suffered from it or friends and family of those affected, had a tendency not to acknowledge it or tell anyone.

Joanie and I discussed it at length on the way back from Denver. I was determined to try to find a way to raise awareness and possibly a little money for research. After all, I loved women and would do anything for them. I thought maybe I could start doing flips on skis again. I hadn't done one intentionally since the Skier Safety Act banned them in the mid-70s. Now that the ban had been lifted, I put together a proposal and submitted it to the Aspen Ski Company for permission. First, I needed to find out if I could still do one.

At the end of the 1999 ski season, the ski company built me a jump on Aspen Mountain. I successfully landed my first front flip in twenty-six years at the age of forty-nine. The ski company gave me the "Okay", so I teamed up with Chris Tucker of Right Now Communications to help me with my campaign and put together my website.

We called it "Loops for Lupus", a name Joanie had come up with. Chris and I spent the summer putting together a 501-c3 non-profit organization and a very sophisticated website. Chris's expertise with websites lay in optimization, ensuring that anyone searching for anything relating to fundraising, Aspen or skiing, would stumble across our website LoopsforLupus.org. The website was full of information about Lupus, my upcoming schedule of events, videos of me doing flips, ways to donate funds to my foundation and a list of my sponsors who came on board to help with my campaign.

My first show and event was scheduled for December 17th, prior to the Christmas holiday. There was a silent auction and an après ski party with live music and myself launching the event with a performance starting at noon. I did seven flips in three hours, not all perfectly, but I survived. I ended up hurting my calf and thought it was just a bruised muscle. My next show wasn't scheduled until my 50th birthday February 28th, so I had a lot of time to heal.

By this time, Ed's mother had passed away so he started coming out to ski with me at Christmas, taking Irving's place. Irving didn't take it lightly. He ranted up and down the halls of the Aspen Mountain Club calling me names which I don't care to repeat. Ed and I exchanged looks and he told me he was willing to let Irving have me back, but I felt it was time to turn Irving over to some other "lucky" pro.

It was a breath of fresh air to ski with Ed for two straight weeks. Ed was a big supporter of my Loops for Lupus effort and offered his services in any way possible. George and Longhorn Steaks was also a big sponsor offering his services in any way as well.

As I approached my next show and birthday event, I was still a little sore in the back of my leg, especially near my knee. I decided to make an appointment with my orthopedist Dr. Mark Purnell just to make sure everything was all right. After reviewing my X-rays and completing a further evaluation, he was unable to find anything wrong, except for one X-ray that he showed me on his lit-up screen.

I looked at it and said, "I broke my leg!"

He remarked, "Yes you did. You broke it right below the tibial plateau and it's healing fine, but try landing on your feet next time."

I asked him what the treatment would have been if I had seen him when I originally hurt it back in December. He told me he would have put me in a cast from my ankle to my hip. I was so glad I hadn't come in. I still had another show to do in a few weeks. Since it was healing nicely, I decided to go for it. Dr. Purnell had operated on my back several years before, knew of my past knee surgery and that I was still performing flips at age 50. He just looked at me and laughed. This was beyond his comprehension.

First flip on skis in 26 years. 1999. Courtesy Chris Hanson

The birthday event was a big success and by this time, we had raised about $12,000. My next show wasn't scheduled until late March during spring break. In the meantime, I had received a call in mid-March around 7:00 a.m. from Bronwyn Sherman representing The Guinness Book of World Records. She told me that they were in the process of completing their website and saw mine, and she was calling to see if there was a possible world record involved in what I was doing.

I told her that if there was any record in this it would probably be the oldest knucklehead and youngest ever to do inverted aerials on skis. She told me that they didn't do anything with the "youngest" category because they didn't want to be responsible for over-zealous parents sending their kids out to do something dangerous. I told her that kids doing flips on skis were a lot younger than I was when I first did mine at age fifteen, but I guaranteed her that they wouldn't be doing them at fifty. She laughed, agreeing with me saying she would get back to me in a few days.

I heard from her shortly thereafter. She explained that no records of this nature existed, but that she would establish one. She asked if I would do as many flips as I could in either a one- or a ten-minute period of time. I took the ten-minute option. I thought I might be able to do six or seven in that time frame.

We had to cancel our spring show due to weather, but still looked for the opportunity to try to establish a world record for health before ski season ended in April. The Aspen Ski Company was very accommodating. They built a jump for me every night during the last week of ski season, but the weather wasn't cooperating. It rained, it snowed, the wind blew or it was foggy. Finally the mountain closed, but I still had two more chances.

The Ski Company had rented the mountain out on closing day for a private party, but that day was too foggy. My last chance was the following day, which was our Employee Appreciation Day. I woke up that morning to a beautiful Colorado blue-sky day. I finally had my chance. The mountain manager, Steve Sewell, had my jump built the night before and scheduled a snowmobile to pick me up after each jump and pull me back up to do another flip. Due to all the delays, Guinness Records couldn't be there in person, so I had to document the whole event. I had my ski school manager video the event, a co-worker operate the stopwatch and one hundred or so of my close friends, who I had worked with for thirty-five years, witness the event.

I asked Scott, the timekeeper, to let me know when I had two minutes left to go. Once I started, I had no concept of time. After the fourth flip, the snowmobile pulled me back up and I heard Scott tell me "One minute twenty-six seconds."

I thought I had time for a few more flips. Due to all the delays after the

fifth one, he said, "One minute forty seconds."

I was thinking that there was something wrong. On the sixth flip my landing was a little short and I sat down. Everyone in the crowd was yelling, "Get up get up!" I got up as Scott came over to me and said, "You've done six in two minutes."

I was thinking that I had just gotten started and had eight more minutes to go. By the time I reached thirteen, the crowd was counting them, my knees were knocking and I was seeing stars. I ended up completing 23 flips in less than ten minutes and I was done! I probably could have finished a few more, but I felt like throwing up and didn't want to get hurt.

I sent the video and the testimonials off to Guinness World Records. Bronwyn called me and congratulated me on my efforts and asked if they could use a trailer of the video for their website. I told her that she could use whatever she wanted and that the package I had sent was theirs to keep. Their website was up and running later that summer. It was amazing to go to the site. The first thing I saw was the video clip of me executing (as the British called it) "Ski Somersaults".

Chris and I decided to continue the fundraising efforts for another year. The on-site donations were increasing slightly, due to the awareness of our campaign and Chris' expertise in website optimization.

Loops for Lupus, 2000. Courtesy Chris Tucker

Tim Charles of Aspen Audio with daughter, Win step up for the cause.

World Record For Health
Winter 2000-2001

Joanie left me just prior to the launch of Loops for Lupus, which had been established in her mom's name for Lupus research. Ed, Chris, and many of my associates and close friends couldn't understand why I continued the fundraiser after she first left. Nobody understood why I was willing to carry it over for one more year. I found myself constantly explaining to people that it was more than just an effort to fundraise for one person.

The reward was that every day I would answer e-mails from sufferers around the world who were familiar with the work I was doing. That alone was a huge reward for me. With all the information and press we had received over the past year, Chris was able to put together an informative website, which at this point was receiving thousands of hits monthly. His effort had really paid off.

That year I only did two shows and one big après ski party just prior to Christmas with live music featuring Jimmy Ibbotson and Bobby Mason. With the help of the town of Aspen, the silent auction made it a great success.

The next show I did was during Presidents' Day weekend. Originally, I was going to establish another world record in ski jumping, this time a one-minute version. The Ski Company planned on building me seven jumps down Little Nell and I was going to attempt to ski from jump to jump doing a flip at each one. The scheduling backfired on us, so we re-enacted the original record at the base of the gondola, with a host of celebrities including Ed Bradley, Dr. Ruth and others. They all signed my ski suit, which now had signatures from Mike Douglas, Robert Wagner, Jill St. John, most of the Bronco football players and more.

The event culminated with a live art auction where Ed Bradley acted as master of ceremonies and auctioned off the art. Once again, the local artists outdid themselves with their donations, while the local restaurants made sure no one went hungry. I had tremendous help and support in making this an extremely successful event. We raised $20,000 and presented it to Virginia Ladd of the American Autoimmune Related Disease Association for Lupus Research.

As the evening came to a close, the last piece of art to be auctioned off was a retro sculpture of myself doing a flip, that a local artist created. While Ed was taking the bids, his soon to be wife, Patricia kept the bidding going by raising it. That was so cool. A person bidding well on it finally yelled out to Ed, "Why do you want it, you've skied with Tommy your whole life?"

Ed replied, "That's why I want it, so that when I don't ski anymore I'll have something to remind me of the fun I had with him."

Patricia outbid everyone and Ed got the sculpture. He closed out the evening with his usual gracious speech congratulating me. After all that excitement, he turned to me and gave me the sculpture. I was absolutely speechless. I thanked him and cried. I'll never forget that night.

Chris and I closed out our Lupus campaign and I went back to staining decks and general house maintenance. It was the stuff I put off and wish I hadn't, because it's always more difficult later. I worked on a couple of my products I had put on the back burner, but neither was ready for the market.

Me "photo
bombing"
Dr. Ruth and
Ed Bradley .

Ready to flip. Aspen Mountain 2001

A great day to close out
"Loops For Lupus."
*Ed, Dr. Ruth, friends,
food, auction and fun!*

Ed and Bonnie's at 11:30 A.M. 2002

Prior to my "Loops for Lupus" campaign, any local article written about Ed Bradley or myself with anything to do with skiing, always referenced me as "Ed Bradley's ski instructor." People would ask us if we were attached at the hip. Ed and I would laugh about this. Although we spent time together in summer and winter, most people were used to seeing us together in winter. They didn't realize that in the summers we would hike, get together for lunch, and be seen together around town at large gatherings or dinner parties. However, in the winter we were totally predictable on the slopes. We had a routine and stuck to it for more than twenty years.

Over the years, we hardly skipped a day on Aspen Mountain, but when we did Ed always felt as if he was missing something. When friends wanted to meet up with him he would say, "Look for us on Aspen Mountain. We're always at Bonnie's at eleven-thirty."

When Ed said 11:30 a.m., he meant 11:30 a.m. We would only be there long enough for soup and a brownie, of which half would go with us, when we left by 12:15 p.m. The crowds dictated our routine; we made every effort to avoid them. The locals referred to these crowds as the "crack of noon club". We generally would hit the slopes by nine. Aspen was a party town

A couple of Ed's buddies chasing us to Bonnie's restaurant. 1995

and everyone started their days later including skiing lunch and dinner. So Ed and I would do everything early. We'd start early, eat early and quit early. That way we were always just ahead of the crowd.

When we did stop to take a break to hit the head, grab a glass of water or just say hi to a friend, strangers would try to approach Ed telling him how much they enjoyed his work and that they had a story for him. It was my job to run interference for him. I would see one coming, look at Ed and say, "Incoming at two o'clock, exit left

Heading for a cold one.

right behind me", and off we would go. On occasion he would get caught, but he was always gracious and appreciative of any comment. When people approached him with some work-related idea, he would kindly tell them to send it to CBS attention Don Hewitt Executive Producer.

When the "Loops for Lupus" campaign was over and people would say something to us on the street Ed would ask me, "Were they talking to you or me?" I looked back at Ed, and in most cases, I told him it was probably him because I had no idea who that person was.

Ed would say, "Yeah, but you've been in the paper much more than I have in the past year and you have a world record."

"Ed," I would say, "You are on T.V. every Sunday evening and at this point everyone in Aspen knows who you are. I'm just a ski instructor." That was the kind of person Ed was, extremely modest and always giving credit rather than taking it.

I was beginning to wonder just how long I would be able to ski at the level I was accustomed to. I wasn't getting any younger and my body was definitely feeling the effects of all that I had put it through during my athletic life. I started to focus more on helping others with their ideas for products rather than inventing my own. I would use my know-how and help them get their products to the next level. I had a great patent attorney Kyle. By now, we had developed not only a business relationship, but a well-defined friendship.

Rapid Rake
2003

I played in a golf tournament that fall and met Mark, a guy on my team who was an appliance repair technician. He was full of ideas and also a very good golfer. About halfway through our round (I had been in and out of sand traps) we were spending more time looking for a rake to clean up the trap, than playing the hole itself, holding players up. At one point he said to me, "Maybe we should just carry a rake in our bag like we do with a ball retriever."

About the time we had finished the round, we began to put the idea of solving the rake problem down on a cocktail napkin. We went into the clubhouse, ordered a couple of beers, tallied up the score and turned it in. Being an inventor myself, and Mark a fix-it guy in the appliance repair business, we sat and talked about this rake idea. Several beers and a dozen cocktail napkins later we had come up with what we called "Rapid Rake".

I went home and did a quick patent search and found out it had been thought of before. Even so, I felt that between the two of us we could design a better more functional gimmick than what I had seen during my search. At a two-day tournament, we spent more time the next day working on our Rapid Rake design than the game itself. We got together a couple of days later to discuss our thoughts and decided to continue with it as a joint venture.

Our rake design was really quite simple. It doubled as a rake and ball retriever. It could be used for cleaning up footprints and divots in a sand trap. The tines on the rake were designed to retrieve a ball from a water hazard without the ball rolling off the rake back into the water. The rake head snapped on the shaft of any golf club and secured itself when slid up to the clubface.

Kyle put me in touch with a company in Denver who did CAD computer assisted design work. Mark and I sat with them and designed it on the computer. Next we took it to Longmont, just north of Denver, to a company who did computer assisted manufacturing and had some prototypes made. Excited about the product, Mark and I asked Kyle to proceed with a provisional patent that would give us a year of protection.

I put together a DVD and sent it out to several golf companies including the obvious ones: Nike and Titleist. In most cases, large companies didn't do much with "outsiders". They tried to keep things in house, which is something I had dealt with before. So the next option would be to manufacture it, go to golf shows, set up a booth and take orders in the traditional marketing setting. Neither Mark nor I were in a position financially to go this route. What appealed to both of us was to try and find someone with a small company with lines of distribution already set up for products like these, who would include Rapid Rake. They would pay us a small royalty similar to what I did with Cush 'n' Carry.

Mark and I worked on this approach during the year we had our provisional patent. I ended up signing off my partnership to him and he ran out of money and energy. "Rapid Rake" fell into what I called the "dead file". It is not uncommon that a product doesn't make it, but you do have to give it a chance.

Even a blind squirrel finds an acorn every now and then!

Tommy Waltner Designs

Tommy Waltner - President

Rapid Rake DVD Point of Purchase

Tommy's Magic Sauces

Over the prior year while developing Rapid Rake I was also working on my mustard recipes. I had developed another mustard, more in line with Mom's original recipe, and a barbecue dipping sauce from the original mustard recipe. Rather than a southern-style-mustard barbecue sauce, I used molasses and catsup with the original mustard base, making it

Tommy's line of Magic Sauces

more of a western-style barbecue sauce. I also developed a honey-mustard vinegar salad dressing marinade to round out my line of Tommy's Magic Sauces. This included a barbecue sauce, salad dressing, and two mustards. I found a company in Denver to manufacture the sauces and Kyle's wife, Janet, designed my labeling.

I've learned through my experiences that I really enjoy starting companies and building businesses, but when winter comes I've got to go back to my real love of skiing, so these companies needed to run themselves for five months a year.

Once Tommy's Magic Sauces got going, it didn't need a lot of help. The company that manufactured and bottled the product helped me get it into Costco in the Denver market, so they could keep making it. I eventually sold it to another small food company that marketed Tommy's Magic Sauces statewide, winning several awards at food shows.

My ski clientele was starting to dwindle slightly. However by this time I had established myself as part of what the Ski Company called the 75-year rule. This was a combination of years of service and age that when totaled 75 would require the instructor to work only 180 hours a year to retain benefits. In my case, my clientele's kids were growing up, going off to college, getting married or just getting too old and participating in other activities.

I had been skiing with a retired chiropractor from Orange County California, Rick Graham, since the mid-90s. Rick had invented the Posture Pump, a back device that I had used and sold to skiers and golfers for years. When I first met Rick and his girlfriend Denise, who ran the Posture Pump Company, we skied together a lot. Rick would stay for a couple of months, while Denise would come and go. As the years passed and they both improved, they didn't need me as much for lessons. Because I worked for them selling their product, we still spent a lot of time together on the snow. As long as Ed and Rick hired me for lessons and I could get a guest or two off the desk at Christmas, 180 hours was doable in order for me to keep my benefits.

That summer at Ed's house in Woody Creek, Colorado, he and Patricia married. Surrounded by their closest friends, it was a special time for them. Not being the anxious type, Ed was full of nervous excitement. Ed had felt his lifestyle of traveling and covering stories all over the world wasn't the kind of lifestyle a wife would put up with, but Patricia was different. She loved Ed and knew how important his work was to him. Patricia was very resourceful. Doing a lot of work in her own right, she kept very busy. They made a great couple and respected each other's space.

Ed and I talked quite a bit about his retiring and spending more time with Patricia. After all, none of us was getting any younger. We discussed going out on top while we were at the top of our game. He compared it to Michael Jordan or John Elway. He and I both knew deep down, easier said than done.

My little design company was busy. A welding business approached me to help develop a shield to protect the eyes when using a mig welder (wire feed welding torch), rather than wearing a protective hood. By this time ,I had a lot of people in my product development "bag of tricks" network. I was able to contact Bob Beody in Michigan, who developed a lot of after-market products and replacement parts for the automotive industry. Having some welding skills himself, he designed a shield that attached to the nozzle of a mig welder that would protect the eyes while doing torch work. While finishing the weld, the shield rotated around to protect the hands.

Filing a provisional patent for the product, I approached Lincoln and Hobart Welding industries. They liked the idea, but felt it would best suit a company who marketed after-market products, rather than a company who manufactured welding machinery. I found two companies who were willing to market the product and distribute through their lines of distribution, which required the business I was working for to manufacture the product itself. They toyed with the idea, but the cost to set up production was more than they wanted to risk. Not more than two months later, a similar product showed up in a Harbor Freight Tools Catalog; not as sophisticated as ours, but manufactured and marketed.

Ed's home in Woody Creek.

My Loft
2005

I stuck my neck out and bought a loft in Basalt that fall before construction even began. I figured if worse came to worse and I couldn't sell my log home in Ruedi I could flip the loft in Basalt. Things were growing rapidly in the valley. I felt it would not only be a good investment, but also the right time for me to start downsizing. I spent a lot of money maintaining a 3000-square-foot house, of which I only used about 800-square-feet.

Ed and I skied a lot that winter. He and Patricia came often, usually around Thanksgiving and Christmas after that about once a month. I also worked a lot that year. The world was in turmoil with all that was happening in the Middle East. We were about to go to war in Iraq, which kept Ed busy traveling.

He finished the ski season in late March, just prior to leaving for a trip back to the Middle East. He hadn't been feeling well this whole trip. We thought he was dealing with acid reflux. He felt uncomfortable after eating and especially when lying down at night to sleep. One of his close doctor friends in town gave him a prescription and advised him to see his doctor in New York before leaving on assignment.

That spring I kept trying to reach him because I was concerned about his condition. He always spent two weeks at the Jazz Festival in New Orleans for as long as I had known him. When I didn't hear from him, I got a little nervous. I had probably left three or four messages for him. I finally received a call back from him in early June. His voice was really rough as he said, "Sorry I didn't get back to you sooner, but I just dodged a bullet."

I was thinking he literally just dodged a real bullet while traveling in a war zone. He continued, "I was at Jazz Fest and this acid condition was so bad I saw a specialist in New Orleans. To make a long story short, I ended up having quintuple heart bypass surgery. Almost didn't make it." It was a tough summer for him. He wasn't able to come to Aspen at all. He had become anemic and wasn't allowed to go to high altitude. I considered going to New York to see him, but between Patricia and his close friends he had plenty of help and support.

I sold my house that Fall. Luckily, the guy who bought it from me asked me if I would house sit for the winter. Because my loft wasn't going to be completed for another year, due to constant construction delays, It worked out perfectly for me.

"Triangle Park has just enough loft for me to flip over."

"Triangle Park Lofts was the perfect place for me to land. Great location. Hip neighborhood. Fitness room. Roof top deck. All the bells and whistles. And 12-foot high ceilings...and I like heights."

— *Tommy Wattner*

Legendary Ski Instructor
Founder, Tommy's Magic Sauces
World-record holder, 23 flips in ten minutes

Triangle Park Lofts. So Hip They Hurt.

FIFTEEN FLOOR PLANS TO CHOOSE FROM | 703 SQUARE FEET TO 1826 SQUARE FEET | STUDIOS | ONE, TWO AND THREE BEDROOMS | $233,000 TO $7

Maxwell vs. Panda Peak
Winter 2006

Tracy Hall, a woman I had skied with for several years in the mid-nineties, married Stan Shopkorn. They had a little boy Maxwell. We all waited until Maxwell was old enough to start skiing. When Maxwell turned 3-1/2, that day finally arrived. We started him in Powder Pandas, a Buttermilk-based ski school for children. Because Maxwell had recently experienced a bad situation at a preschool in Florida and had developed separation anxiety, Tracy asked me to teach him to ski.

He picked it up pretty quickly. We skied Panda Peak, the learning area at the base of Buttermilk, with the assistance of a Hula-Hoop and a bamboo pole. I did all I could to trick him with that pole. We started out side-by-side holding the pole. As we skied down, I slowly pushed the pole toward him until he was holding it in the middle, then I would let go and he had no idea that he was skiing by himself using the pole for balance. Once he learned to stop in a snowplow, he didn't need the pole any more.

By the end of five days of ski lessons, he had skied Panda Peak all by himself. I knew through experience that kids don't develop muscle memory that early in life. The bicycle theory doesn't come into play at that age, so we would have to wait to see the following year how he was going to progress.

It had been a rough ski year for Ed. He was now able to come to high altitude, but had to carry oxygen with him and sleep with an oxygen system in his house. When we skied he carried a blood/oxygen meter which he would attach to his finger to check his blood oxygen level. If it went below 90%, he would pull out the oxygen and take 20 hits or so. As he put it, it was a pain in the ass, but at least he was skiing.

He had been worried that he would have to sell his Woody Creek house and stop skiing, but that was no longer the case. He told me earlier that year that with all the health issues he was going through the doctors had discovered he had Leukemia. He didn't want me to say anything. Although it wasn't the kind of blood cancer that would send him to his grave, he didn't feel everyone needed to know everything about his health.

By the end of the season he was back skiing as if nothing had happened. With his strength improved and his oxygen levels close to normal, he was looking forward to hiking a lot that summer and skiing the following winter like he had done in the past. He wanted to ski 30 days and rip it up.

MAX - 0   PANDA PEAK - 1   But from the looks of his support team, he'll be fine... tired but fine.

Tracy, Maxwell and me... whooped!

Let's try it with a hula hoop.

Like the pole better do you?

157

Ed Passes
2006

Moving out of my huge log home in Ruedi was no easy task. Not knowing where I was going until my loft was finished left me no other choice than to move all of my stuff, and I mean all 3500-square-feet of it, into storage. Even though I was moving into just a thousand square feet of living area, I wasn't comfortable getting rid of anything until I could see how things were going to fit. Tom the new owner wasn't moving into the house until August, so I still had some time to move out.

I was looking forward to downsizing and not having to paint, stain, repair winter damage, water and mow the yard, and all of the other things that needed to be done as a homeowner. There was always something to do. If I put it off, I wished I hadn't because when I would get around to it, it seemed it was always more work than I had bargained for.

When August came, I handed the keys to Tom with a small tear in my eye. I was going to miss my log cabin in the woods. At the same time, I was happy for Tom, who was really excited about his next chapter in life.

Dave my stepdad had passed away two summers before at his ranch in Wyoming. His wife Betty had invited me up to hang out, help her around the ranch, and fish and golf until my loft was finished. I thought I'd be lucky to move in before ski season, so I went to the ranch for a month and then to Santa Monica to visit Greg and Patty Behr, Rick and Denise. I surfed and caught up with friends from June Lake as well as people I had met skiing in Aspen.

I returned to Aspen in late October, my loft was a couple of months away from being finished. Fortunately, I was able to house sit near my former cabin in Ruedi. Tom was still getting settled in, so I helped him quite a bit. By this time the leaves had fallen off the trees. With winter just around the corner, I was beginning to get excited about ski season.

On November 9th I was having breakfast in Basalt, when a ski instructor I had taught with for thirty years called me and asked what I was doing. It was a little strange because he never called just to chitchat. I told him I was just finishing breakfast.

"What's up?"

"Are you sitting down?"

"Yes."

"Your best friend just passed away."

"Who?" I responded in panic.

"Ed Bradley."

My stomach hit bottom. "How do you know?"

"I just saw it on CNN."

"How did he die?"

"Leukemia."

I knew it was true, and started to cry. He asked if I was okay. All I could say was, "That wasn't supposed to kill him." I went out and just sat in my car for an hour. I didn't know what to do. I had lost friends and loved ones before, but this really hurt. I felt as though someone had just ripped my heart out. I tried to contact Patricia, Jimmy Buffett, Dick Butera and several of Ed's dearest friends, but it was impossible. I spoke with Ester, a woman Ed had worked with at CBS and who I had known for 20 years. She skied in Aspen a lot, had a condo there and was my inside source to Ed whenever I tried to contact him and couldn't reach his personal secretary. I finally talked to Natasha, Patricia's sister, who stayed in touch with me to let me know when the memorial service was going to be. I wasn't going to miss that for anything in the world.

The memorial service was held on Tuesday, November 21st at the Riverside Church in New York City. I had never gone to New York before, other than Lake Placid in 1980. I called Tracy to let her know I was coming. She already knew about Ed, everybody did. She told me not to worry, that she and Stan would take care of everything for me. I just needed to let her know when I was arriving at LaGuardia.

Tracy and Stan were wonderful to me. Their driver picked me up at the airport and took me to their home in Manhattan. They booked a hotel room close by, feeling that I would be more comfortable there than at their place.

The next day, their driver picked me up at my hotel and took me to the church where the service was held. I was totally blown away. It was a celebration of Ed's life like nothing I had ever seen before. The music, the tribute by Don Hewitt, Steve Croft and all of the people who worked directly with Ed were there. Many people gave remembrances: Bill Cosby, and Ed's godson, Cordell Whitlock, who I had taught to ski, Jimmy Buffett, the Wynton Marsalis Band, and Aaron and Art Neville just to name a few. Charlayne and Ron Gault delivered the eulogy. A lot of Ed's friends, who I had spent time with in Aspen came, so I wasn't alone.

From the church we walked several blocks to the Terrace Restaurant on the Hudson for lunch and spirits to celebrate Ed's life. Ester grabbed me and introduced me to many of Ed's colleagues. When I met them most said, "So

"If you don't want it printed, don't let it happen."

Aspen Daily News

INSIDE TODAY'S PAPER — Time Out

aspendailynews.com

The Roaring Fork Valley's only independent and locally owned newspaper

Printed on Recycled Paper | FRIDAY, NOVEMBER 10, 2006 | VOL. 29 #130

Aspen remembers its '60 Minutes' man

Ed Bradley lived a down-to-earth life

By Troy Hooper
Aspen Daily News Staff Writer

Someone will be missing when ski instructor Tommy Waltner rides the gondola up Aspen Mountain this Thanksgiving: CBS news icon Ed Bradley.

While the rest of the nation remembers the award-winning television journalist as the smooth, black anchor on "60 Minutes" who beamed into their living rooms for more than a quarter century, his closest friends in Colorado are summoning up images of a down-to-earth individual who loved to hike and ski.

"New York was his work place and Aspen was his play place," said Waltner, who called Bradley his client and comrade for 26 years. "We used to ski 30 to 40 days a season together. To be perfectly honest, Ed was my career. He and I used to joke about it. He was my lifeline. Ed was much more than a client. He was like my best friend. It won't be the same skiing Aspen Mountain without Ed Bradley up there. He was a fixture on that mountain for so long."

Until his death on Thursday, it wasn't public knowledge that Bradley had been suffering from lymphocytic leukemia. But his confidants in Aspen knew.

"He told me he had leukemia several years ago," said Pitkin County Sheriff Bob Braudis, who received a phone call from a Bradley relative at 4 a.m. Thursday informing

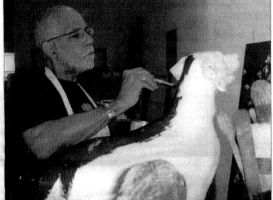

Ed will be missed.

you are Tommy." I was surprised to meet so many of Ed's co-workers who knew of me, but had never met me. I felt very comfortable and welcome in an environment where I might have felt out of place.

President Bill Clinton made a surprise appearance at the service. While sitting with a close friend from Aspen, Rob Van Pelt, and reminiscing Ed's life over a glass of red wine, in walked President Clinton. He entered the Terrace Restaurant with a swarm of secret service agents, only to have friends and fans approach him. He looked over and saw Rob and me toasting our red wine to Ed. Rob was wearing his signature big, beautiful, black cowboy hat. I was mourning Ed's death and was sure President Clinton was thinking we must be a couple of Republicans because Rob and I just sat there while everyone else crowded around him seeking autographs, taking pictures and shaking hands. Clinton didn't hesitate to walk over to us and shake our hands. As he walked away, I looked at Rob and said, "At least we stood up!" We both laughed.

My plans were to fly out of New York on Thanksgiving Day to avoid the rush, but Tracy and Stan wouldn't have it. They wanted me to stay and have Thanksgiving with them.

Reflecting

Wow! New York City! Ed had always invited me to come, but I never did. Now I wished I could have enjoyed it with him. I had no idea it was so beautiful and overwhelming. I've skied with a lot of people over the years who worked and played in the city, but to see it is the only way one can understand what others are talking about. The streets seem so narrow and the buildings so tall.

As the driver was taking me back to La Guardia for my flight home, I kept thinking I would really like to come back and see it under different circumstances and be able to take my time exploring. Tracy and Stan were tremendous hosts and did so much to make my short stay enjoyable and memorable, from the time I arrived, through Thanksgiving dinner, to my return back home.

I couldn't help but think of my relationship with Ed and how sad it was going to be to ski without him. He was my career. I knew I just couldn't continue to move forward as though he were just another client who had come and gone. We had spent more than 30 days a year skiing together, not to mention summers. He had become an integral part of my life and was like family. I remembered so much. The small things, things that didn't seem so important at the time, but now that they were gone reappeared as thoughts that were so very special.

As I arrived at the airport 2-1/2 hours early, it reminded me of Ed and how he started using NetJet for work, something he hadn't done until after 9-11. Prior to that time he had thought it was too extravagant for a working-man of his character. He didn't want to be the only journalist with 60 Minutes flying from interview to interview in a private jet.

My mind wouldn't stop, all I wanted to do was remember my friend. I bought a book and a magazine anything to try to get my mind on something else. Even those made me think of Ed and my mom telling me I should write a book about all of my amazing life stories. I often retold them to friends over the years to help me remember. As my mom would say, "I don't know how you could write a book when you can't even read one." She was right. Every time I tried to read my mind would be off somewhere else, in this case somewhere with Ed. I don't know if I was daydreaming or if my mind just wasn't processing what I was reading. I did know that my thoughts of Ed were so strong, that it was useless to try to read anything.

I thought about the conversations we had about going out on top.

You can't have enough of these at a time like this.

ED BRADLEY

Tommy,
Hope all is well.
I'll see you in April
Regards

ED BRADLEY

Dear Tommy,
Who said 13 was an unlucky number? This season was certainly better than last both in number of days and quality of skiing.
Many thanks for your help in making this a great winter and spring.
And, thanks for the book —
All the best,

ED BRADLEY

Tommy,
Many thanks. We made the best of what we had.
Your buddy,

162

That's exactly what Ed had done. When he left us he was at the top of his game. This was evident talking with the people he had worked with at his memorial service. He will be remembered as one of the greatest journalists of his time.

When I returned home my loft was finished. Moving in helped me get my mind off Ed. He really wanted to see my new place when it was done. I know he would have liked it. My architect had also done remodels for Ed over the years on his Woody Creek home.

Just before Christmas, I finished moving in and was ready to return to work. Before that could happen, I had to make a couple of laps for Ed on his favorite runs: Copper Bowl and Spar Gulch.

Remembering Ed Bradley
2007

At some point over the course of the winter I was contacted by most, if not all of the local magazines, wanting to know as much as possible about Ed his life and skiing in the Roaring Fork Valley. "Remembering Ed Bradley" was the theme. All that was written about him was nothing short of what a remarkable down to earth person he had been and how generous he had been with his time with everyone he knew. I felt extremely lucky to have spent so much time with him skiing, hiking and being there when he needed someone to share his concerns.

Tracy and Maxwell skied a couple of times that winter. On their first trip in February, Maxwell, now four years old, didn't remember much of his previous time on skis, which was to be expected. However, within a couple of days he was skiing most of the easy blue runs at Buttermilk with little assistance. When we skied at Snowmass on his last day he did quite well, until he got tired. Since I never knew exactly when that would happen I always carried a harness with a leash so I could support him from behind. Then he could lead me down the mountain without going too fast.

When Tracy and Maxwell returned in March for spring break it was a whole different story. This time Max remembered much of what he had learned earlier. We pretty much started where we had left off. By the end of that trip, Maxwell had skied all four Aspen Ski Areas: Buttermilk, Snowmass, Aspen Mountain and Highlands. The "Power of Four" at four years old! It was pretty impressive for the little guy and I had a great feeling of accomplishment for both of us.

When he got tired, I got the harness.

164

One proud mom with one tired little boy. The Power of Four at four. 2007

Chrysler Corporation

As I became more involved helping other companies patent and market their products, I noticed similarities in their approach. We experienced the same feeling, "This is my baby and I have my own way of raising it."

One company I got involved with was a design company working on an after-market convertible top for CJ 5's, CJ 7's and Wrangler Jeeps for Chrysler. Starting this project when Lee Iacocca was CEO, the man responsible for saving Chrysler, they had been working on this great idea for several years.

Since I had skied with the president of sales for Chrysler during a "King of the Mountain" ski event in Aspen, I offered to try to get my foot in the door. Their connection was Lee Iacocca. Because they were scared someone would steal their idea, it took them way too long to get through the protection process. By the time they had gotten it together to produce a working prototype, Lee Iacocca had left Chrysler. The company was no longer interested. My client had a great product with no interest from a major manufacturer. By this time Jeep had changed to the Rubicon model, while their prototype had been developed for the CJ and Wrangler models.

They were out of money and didn't have a way of marketing it as an after-market product for Napa or any of the major after-market-auto outlets. It reminded me of some of my earlier products like Cool-Apse: better to take a risk early on and to give the product a chance to survive.

Timing is essential in determining the success or failure of a product in the marketplace. By the time you've jumped through all of the necessary hoops to protect the product, someone else may have come along with a similar design and gotten to the market just a few months prior. In the Chrysler case, by the time the design company was ready to move, Chrysler had already come out with a new model with a different body style.

You can only give people advice based on your own experiences. In many cases, egos get in the way preventing timely success. If someone wants help, I am willing to give advice based on my experience, but at a certain point I need to charge a fee. It's like teaching people to ski. They won't get anything out of it unless they pay for it. It's just human nature. If you have to pay for something you'll make sure you get something in return. You just can't give your expertise away.

Age and Como
2008

It was getting a little harder each year to reach the goal of 180 hours per season to keep my benefits. It was getting more important to get lessons off the desk and every year there were fewer lessons to be divided up between instructors needing work. That year at Christmas I got lucky.

Two guests from Canada, Jeff Kirby and Olga, his fiancée, needed an instructor for three weeks. I was one of the few instructors who was willing to ski for a three-week period with guests from a culture that generally didn't tip. I personally didn't care about the tip because the more work I had, the easier it would be to attain the hours needed to keep my benefits.

Jeff was an international developer who traveled into third-world countries to help rebuild their culture. He met Olga while developing a city in Romania. Since he had grown up in Toronto, he was a great skier — unlike Olga who had only skied a few times in Austria and Switzerland. We had great fun and I spent most of my time working with Olga. The "squeaky wheel" gets the grease, one might say. Jeff was extremely generous, paying for sit-down lunches every day in the nicest restaurants, acting very European and making sure that most of the attention was on his wife to be.

About two weeks into the vacation, Olga learned that she was pregnant. Not feeling great and not wanting to jeopardize her pregnancy, she opted out of skiing. That left the third week of their trip for Jeff and me to rip it up and we did! We had a blast. Although Jeff didn't want to call it quits for the season, he had to get back to Romania to finish his project.

Not expecting anything at all on our final day together, he took me into town for lunch at Mezzaluna. He asked if I would consider coming to Europe at the end of the season to ski in Austria for a couple of days. Afterwards, we could go to his place in Lake Como in northern Italy and stay in his villa on the lake with all expenses paid. He added that I could bring my girlfriend.

I looked at Jeff and said, "Of course! Do you think I'm nuts or something?" Exchanging e-mails, he told me his secretary would contact me soon. My girlfriend Maggie was in India at the time. I couldn't wait for her to come back to share the news that we were going to Italy!

As spring approached, I was beginning to think this would be one of those promises that sounded like a good idea at the time without the intention of following through. We did stay in touch, and in early April I received an e-mail telling me that skiing wasn't going to happen because Olga was having some problems with her pregnancy. He went on to say that if we wanted, his secretary would send us our plane tickets and we could stay in his villa on the lake with a driver and a cook at our service.

Maggie and I left for Italy in mid-April. We were both very excited and didn't know what to expect. While we were waiting for our bags at the Milan airport, I looked at Maggie and said, "This trip is either going to be really cheap or really expensive." We walked out of the baggage terminal and sure enough there was a driver holding a sign with my name on it. Maggie gave me a big kiss. With a giant smile on my face I said, "Let the trip begin!"

We had a wonderful ten-day stay that included reading, relaxing, eating, drinking red wine and acting like tourists. When Maggie and I arrived back in the states, we had spent half the amount of money we'd expected to spend. Jeff and Olga had a baby girl at Christmas and named her Elizabeth Aspen.

We got back the day before ski season ended. Maggie had an important business appointment. My end of the season party was the next day, which was a lot of fun. I always enjoyed that party. In many cases, it would be the last time I would see my friends until the next ski season. It was also the day I had set my world record for health.

Villa del Balbianello. Built in 1787, a favorite for filmmakers. Star Wars & Casino Royale filmed here.

Lake Como from Jeff and Olga's Villa

Ed's Bench and Snowboarding
2009-2010

Aspen Mountain is a place full of shrines in memory of people like John Denver, Elvis Presley, Jerry Garcia and many more. That's why I felt it would be more appropriate to honor Ed with a bench rather than a shrine. While at the party I bumped into Mike, the chief operating officer, and asked if it would be okay if I had a bench placed in memory of Ed somewhere on the mountain. Mike wasn't too keen on the idea. He thought there were too many shrines and memorabilia cluttering up the mountain. My comment was, "Yeah, but Ed spent 25 years skiing and hiking here and the likes of Elvis and Jerry Garcia never set foot in Aspen." Mike looked at me and said, "Okay. I'll look the other way on this one."

I talked to Vaughn Shafer, a welding friend ,who despite being very busy at the time, came up with a beautiful design. I explained to him that there was no hurry as we had all summer, which gave me time to figure out where to put it. As summer came to an end and Vaughn completed the bench, I had it powder coated in a metallic red finish. It was stunning! I did this because of a story Ed had once told me.

While shopping in an antique store in town several years before, Ed had purchased a dining room table at Little Bear Antiques. The chairs hadn't come in yet. One afternoon when Ed and I had finished skiing, he asked me to come to the store with him and see if the chairs had arrived. Finding the owner busy, we decided to mill around. Hanging from the wall was an old Flexible Flyer sled. Ed looked at me and said that when he was a kid he would have killed for one of those. Growing up in Philadelphia on any snowy day he and his buddies would go to the local park with cafeteria trays or cardboard or any makeshift sled that would slide on the snow. One day, one of his friend's showed up with a brand new bright red Flexible Flyer. When he got home he begged his mom for one.

As a child Ed never did get his red sled, so I had a plaque engraved and put it on the bench. It read: "Ed's Red Sled." The bench would have a permanent home at Bonnie's Restaurant on Aspen Mountain. We dedicated Ed's bench right before Christmas. There was a large turnout, including Patricia and many of Ed's closest friends. We toasted with champagne and talked about the fun Ed had skiing on Aspen Mountain. The bench remains at Bonnie's today.

Meanwhile, Maxwell was now seven years old and beginning to explore other on-snow options. The X-Games, now in its 12th year on Buttermilk Mountain, had Maxwell's curiosity in high gear. That year Tracy brought him to Aspen in late January so he could witness the competition live. It's an event that really has to be seen in person to feel the full effects of how crazy and talented these athletes are, whether they are on snowmobiles, skis or snowboards. The stunts they do in the air are absolutely spectacular.

Tracy and I wanted to try to keep Maxwell skiing as long as possible, but we both knew one day he was going to want to snowboard. Well that day had come! Maxwell asked me if I had ever tried it and I told him the story of when I had.

"You see Maxwell, the first time I ever snowboarded goes back to June Lake in the late 60s early 70s. It was called snow surfing. A guy from southern California showed up at June Lake with a small piece of wood shaped like a surfboard. A small fin ran along the bottom back of the board with a hole at its tip where a rope was tied to hang on to. A piece of ribbed rubber attached to the middle of the board acted as bindings where snow boots, usually Sorrels, were placed."

My first attempt at "modern" snowboarding was in 1985. Every year I was required to take mandatory training necessary for insurance requirements. Time was running out as it did every year. There were always plenty of pros needing more training. We were given the choice to either sit in the Ritz Carlton Hotel (now the St. Regis) to listen to a workman's compensation seminar for two days or go to Buttermilk to take a snowboard clinic. I opted to be outside.

A bunch of us showed up at Buttermilk for the clinic. It was a pretty colorful site. I had my ski boots on with a carving board and bindings. Others had Sorrells with a soft binding set up, which was good for more all around and freestyle boarding. My buddy, Matt from Vail ,who had been teaching in Aspen for a couple of years showed up dressed in bubble wrap. He knew he would fall a lot learning to snowboard. More than that, he was a funny character and was always good for a laugh. Before the lesson started, Matt and I decided to make a run on Panda Peak — about as steep as a pool table. I looked like I knew what I was doing, but didn't. Matt looked like the Michelin Man all decked out in bubble wrap. Loading the lift was interesting, as we had to stand sideways rather than straight when on skis. Matt sat down and all you could hear was pop, pop, pop!

I laughed the whole way up the lift. Thanks to all the surfing and skateboarding I did growing up I didn't fall getting off. Matt fell and "popped" a couple of times. As we boarded down, I did fine until it was time to stop at the bottom. I hit and broke a 4x4 board used for forming groups into classes. Matt, who was also unable to stop, sat down and rolled a time or two, creating a cacophony of popping. I figured it out rather easily due to my early and ongoing experiences with skiing, skateboarding and surfing.

When Maxwell came back in February for Presidents' Day weekend, he tried snowboarding. Kids either really like it and want to continue because their friends snowboard, or don't like all the falling and sitting down for the first couple of days until they get the hang of it. This was Maxwell's experience.

When he returned in March for spring break it was time for me to find another pro who could teach him the fine art of rails, half pipes and "trick park" etiquette, as Maxwell called it. It worked out well. Tracy and I had bad knees and skied around the jumps, bumps and rails to watch and video Maxwell. "A chip off the old block," I thought.

Summer arrived and Maggie and I bought a tent trailer. I still had my little Hobie Cat up at Ruedi, so we camped and sailed a lot. Ruedi was a great spot to get away for a couple of days in the middle of the week to camp, sail, hike and just kickback and enjoy the water. Later that summer, I bought a cute little motorcycle, not to ride but as an investment. The girl who owned it was leaving the valley. Her ex-boyfriend had bought it for her and she no longer wanted it. It was a brand new 650cc Suzuki Boulevard and looked

INSIDER | *profile*

LEFT TO RIGHT:
Tommy Waltner and Ed's wife, Patricia Blanchet, on Ed's Red Sled; Tommy and Ed showing off on Aspen Mountain; carvings on the bench at Bonnie's.

Ed's Red Sled

One of the many stories the media used to celebrate Ed's life.
Ed's "Red Sled" Memorial Bench sits on the deck at Bonnie's Restaurant.

just like a Harley Davidson Sportster with only 381 total miles on it. I paid $2,500 for it thinking I could make a quick $1,000. Unfortunately, summer was about over and the few people interested didn't want to store it for the winter.

I got a call on December seventh from a guy I had met earlier from Paonia, Colorado that was interested in buying it for his wife for Christmas. I hadn't started it up for a month or so, and felt if he was going to drive over from Paonia I'd better try to start it. I had put a total of 18 miles on it since I bought it. It would start, but it would cut out as soon as I tried to give it gas. I thought it was flooded so I pushed it out of the parking garage to let it air out in the autumn sunshine. I left it for an hour or so and watched some football and had a couple of beers while it dried out.

When I went back down to see if it would run, nothing had changed. I walked it back over to the entrance of the parking garage putting the kickstand down so I could push the keypad to open the garage. The kickstand failed. The bike fell on top of me ,knocking out my four front lower teeth, cutting my mouth and splitting open the back of my head, just short of fracturing my skull. An employee at a restaurant in my building called 911 and off to the hospital I went.

Anytime 911 is called to the scene, not only does an ambulance show up, but the police and sometimes the fire department as well. The police questioned me in the ambulance and thirty minutes or so after arriving at the hospital, while being stitched up, a policewoman wrote me a ticket for driving under the influence. I refused a breath test and a blood test. For one, I wasn't driving and I was spitting blood from my mouth where I had knocked my teeth out and cut my upper lip to my chin. The charges were eventually dismissed.

Since I didn't have any clients coming for Christmas, rather than try to get some lessons off the private lesson desk, I decided I'd be better off recovering inside instead of teaching outside in the elements.

TIAs and Motorcycle Accident
Winter 2011

Rick and Denise came out to ski in January. Tracy and Maxwell skied during Presidents' Day weekend and March spring break. For the most part, I was struggling a bit with balance and my thought processes weren't as keen as they should have been. When Tracy arrived in March with Maxwell, I would normally get instructors for her staff and friends. This time I seemed to be a little confused and lacking some organizational skills, which I'm usually very good at.

As summer approached, I didn't feel much better. My brother Willie took me to Vail to see a neurologist. He ran several tests including an EEG (electronic brain wave test), which later showed several TIAs (transient ischemic attacks or mini strokes/seizures) from severe contusion to the front left of my brain from the motorcycle episode.

Later in Autumn, while polishing my wood floors in my sock feet at around 8:30 p.m., I slipped and fell landing on a doorstopper. I couldn't get to my phone or my front door. The next morning, I realized I had injured myself pretty severely. I didn't just bruise my hip as I had hoped. Slithering like a snake I struggled to get to the living room, found my phone and realized my front door was locked. I called a locksmith, who had a master key to the lofts in the building where I lived. He showed up, unlocked my door and called the Basalt police. The police showed up with an ambulance and once again, off to the hospital I went. I was put on a morphine pump in the ambulance. The next thing that I remember is waking up to Dr. St. John, from Aspen Orthopedic Associates, standing over me telling me I had hit the door-stop perfectly, fracturing my hip and breaking my femur.

I ended up with several screws in my femur and a plate from my femur to my hip. I was able to start rehab immediately. By mid-October, when I graduated from my walker, my old friend Wheels lent me a beautiful handmade knotty pine cane. Around Christmas time, when I no longer relied on the cane, I called Wheels to tell him I was going to return it to him. He said, "I don't want it. You keep it. That thing is bad luck!" I laughed and said I would hang on to it for us.

EEGs and Alcohol
2012

In early January, I was talking with my primary care physician about my TIAs. My balance still wasn't right and my memory wasn't the same. Granted, I wasn't getting any younger, but I was still concerned. Dr. Susan Inscore, who had been my doctor for nearly 20 years, wanted me to see Dr. Allen, a neurologist in Basalt, who could explain my EEG results. Susan thought my hip and femur episode had been caused by a seizure.

Dr. Allen showed me my brain scan images on her computer. I asked her what the star-like lights were and she said they were lesions from the TIAs. I immediately asked her if she could tell me what part of my brain was affected. She told me balance, speech, memory and a few other areas. I was blown away by the technology; she explained this type of diagnostics had been around for a while.

Both Susan and Dr. Allen were concerned with my alcohol use. After seeing the images of my brain, I could understand why. I wasn't too worried about the marijuana, but my alcohol use was another thing. Cutting back would be "easier said than done." I cut back on both, but wished I could stop drinking all together. My liver enzymes were out of balance. Being hurt and unable to ski, I was drinking things I didn't normally drink and drinking more than I normally would.

Since Rick was recovering from stomach surgery, he and Denise didn't ski that winter. Tracy and Maxwell came for the X-Games in late January and Presidents' weekend in February. I met Tracy and Maxwell every morning to handle the logistics of four ski instructors, Tracy's guests and all of the equipment. Bummed I couldn't ski, I still took care of everything for them. Meeting Tracy for lunch wasn't the same. When Tracy and Maxwell returned in March for two weeks I kept trying to convince myself that if there were a season to miss, this would be the one. With little precipitation since Presidents' weekend, the snow wasn't very good.

On March 22nd, they skied Snowmass and as usual I met all of them for lunch. I have little memory of the events that followed. I remember arriving at the parking garage and then being in the Pitkin County Jail, but nothing in between. Evidently, I had hit a couple of parked cars in the garage after lunch, where I had had a glass and a half of wine.

Two weeks later, after discovering all of this with my attorney, parts of it began to come back to me, almost as if I was a blackout drinker. I was so grateful not to have hurt myself or anyone else. From that point on, I decided I was done with drinking and determined not to drive again until I fully understood the seizures. I spent the summer in court-ordered sobriety programs, which I needed and were good for me. I also got as strong as I could because I didn't want to miss another ski season.

Mom Passes

A few years ago when my mom wasn't doing well, my siblings and I decided it would be best for her to live in an assisted-living facility. Her dementia had turned to Alzheimer's, while her osteoporosis, which she suffered from since her 40s, was getting the best of her. None of us thought she would make it through the year.

Mom died December 7th, 2012. Despite the fact that I thought I had prepared myself, I realized there really was no way to do that. The things that started going through my mind were overwhelming. For one thing, now I was an orphan with no living relatives other than my brothers and sisters. I thought of Moey and Bop my grandparents and how much they had meant to me throughout my life, even to this day. I thought about Aunt Bea, Bops' sister and Uncle Haha (Harland Taylor) whose name "HaHa" evolved when we were children, because none of us could pronounce Harland. He and Aunt Bea weren't able to have children of their own and always thought of Mom as a daughter. Good to all of us, unfortunately they had only lived a little longer than Moey and Bop.

Uncle HaHa was Vice President Nixon's personal physician and a well-decorated medical officer in the army. He told some great stories of the bombing of Pearl Harbor during World War II when he and Aunt Bea had been stationed there. While Uncle HaHa traveled the world, he acquired one of the largest carved elephant collections. Many of them can still be seen to this day at the Smithsonian Institute.

It's sad when it takes losing a loved one to remember so many good things that will be missed. It also reminded me of how important it is to spend as much time as you can with the ones you truly love, especially as one gets older. I had a similar feeling when Ed passed away, only as it should be.

Retirement

As Christmas approached that winter, skiing was limited. Only the Little Nell chair and Bell Mountain lifts were open on Aspen Mountain. The snow on top wasn't good enough to open the gondola. My Christmas booking cancelled and went to Hawaii instead. If clients weren't coming to Aspen, they had to make plans to go where snow wasn't an issue. The thought of trying to get work off the desk wasn't appealing to me. Little snow and no skiers meant no work so I didn't pick up my uniform or employee pass and opted for my years of service pass instead, just to see if I could even ski.

I called Tracy and told her I wouldn't be skiing in my uniform with her during her February and March trips. She immediately asked, "What does that mean?"

I explained, "Nothing really, I'll still handle all your arrangements for Maxwell your guests and whatever needs you have including house rental and ski instructors." Tracy and I had been skiing together for nearly 20 years. She skied as well as most instructors. I would have been disappointed in myself if she didn't. She was totally okay with it and commented that now she could buy ski clothes for me. We both laughed.

Dr. Rippy
2013

Rick and Denise came out the first week of January. It was so nice to be skiing again. Both Rick and I had missed a full year of skiing. Denise had thought it was R.I.P. for both of us as far as skiing went. The R.I.P. quickly evolved into "Rip" because we were both skiing very well. Denise can be extremely funny and before I knew it she dubbed me, "Dr. Rippy and Mr. Waltner". Every time Dr. Rippy was having too much fun, Mr. Waltner would tighten the reigns.

We had a lot of fun. Rick wanted to ski powder and since January is the least snowy month he left with plans to come back after Presidents' Day weekend. Tracy and Maxwell also came for Presidents' weekend and I was having tons of fun being back in my element. I've been so fortunate to have long-time clients who have become close friends — that includes all of my clients.

Dr. Rippy on Aspen Mountain. 2014

The Accident
March 2013

Rick came back at the end of February as planned. With plenty of powder on the slopes we ripped it up. On March 1st, the day after my 63rd birthday, Rick and I were out early skiing powder as we had done the previous couple of days. Being tired, we decided to go down into town for lunch. Just short of getting to the bottom, another skier hit me. He went down and came out of both skis, while I battled not to fall. It's hard to knock me down on skis. When I did come down I landed on my shoulder. Rick couldn't believe what he had just seen. There was no reason for this guy to run right into me. Nobody was around; the light was good; the snow was good. It just didn't make sense to either of us that someone would just plow right into me.

I was hurt. The mountain manager Peter King, whom I have known since 1973, had been skiing right behind Rick and me. He stopped and called the patrol. I was thinking that I had been bumped into accidentally, but I'd never been hit like that before. The guy who hit me started walking back up to get his skis and asked, "Are you alright?"

I said, "No I'm not alright! What were you doing skiing that close to me?" He responded, "Well…"

Rick immediately said, "Well What?" The guy went on to say he had taught at Snowmass up until a few years ago and understood the skier safety code that the downhill skier has the right of way and apologized to me.

The patrol showed up and Peter asked me if I wanted a toboggan to which I replied, "I've never been in a toboggan and I don't plan on getting into one now." I had been skiing for 59 years and teaching for 44 without any of

I never thought I'd have to get in one of these. Better yet, thankfully, none of my students during my 46 year career had to. That, I'm proud of!

my students or myself having to get in one. I was extremely proud of that. Unfortunately, I was so nauseous and in pain that I chose to go down the last three hundred yards in the sled. When the patrol got me down to the bottom, Peter offered to get his car and take me to the hospital. They got me out of the toboggan and sat me on a fence railing while we waited for Peter. As I was sitting there I heard a loud voice saying, "Tommy, Tommy! Wake up!" I asked the patrol, "How long was I out?" He told me only a few seconds. I responded with, "I want to go back to where I was." I think I had just had an out of body experience. Peter showed up and off to the hospital we went. (Perhaps this book should have been called "Off to the Hospital.")

En route, Peter and I discussed how the entire dynamics of skiing had changed since shaped skis were introduced. It used to be that you would try to stay as far away from other skiers as possible. If you fell, you would slide ten or twenty feet. However, now everyone has edges, so when you fall or get too much edge you lose the ability to finish your turn and end up in the trees or hitting other skiers. Everyone has edges now — whether they know how to use them or not.

I was wheeled into the emergency room and undressed. They took X-rays of my arm and pelvis area. In battling not to fall, I had pulled every muscle in my groin area. The doctors wanted to make sure all the hardware from my hip and femur were still in place. I was rolled back to my curtain-clad room where my I.V. was filled with pain relievers. I was in shock. I tried to explain to the nurses that I didn't want any mind-altering drugs. I had been

Since Ed's passing I often wondered when this day was coming. I was hoping the circumstances would have been different.

sober for almost a year, but the nurses apparently knew best. I started to feel like a "puppy in a pickup." When the on-call orthopedic surgeon came in, I wished I WAS that "puppy in a pickup." Dr. von Stade was young, pretty, and sweet. She told me I had fractured my humerus and wanted me to come to her office the following Monday.

Peter was nice enough to take me home and go to the pharmacy for me. When I hobbled in my front door, I knew exactly where Wheels's "bad luck" cane was. I opened the closet and said to the cane, "Maybe you are bad luck, but I'm certainly glad you're here!" At that point I knew I wasn't going to teach skiing any more. I felt as though I should trade my skis in for a buggy whip and some wooden teeth; I felt so old and beat up.

Rehab

After I started rehab and was feeling a little better, I realized there wasn't any way I was going to stop skiing. I was only 63 years old. If Klaus Obermeyer, one of my sponsors for Loops for Lupus, could do it at 90+ years, I couldn't be done yet. My first rehab consisted of stretching my groin area and simple range of motion exercises for my upper arm. As my groin area improved, Dr. von Stade questioned why I was still using the cane. The MRI on my back revealed that I had two fractures in my sacrum, which explained my pain and the likely reason for the cane.

People were opening doors for me, stopping in the crosswalks and asking if there was anything they could do. In the back of my mind I could hear Wheels saying, "This thing is bad luck." Eventually I was able to put the cane back in the closet. By this time I was dealing with a lazy rotator cuff injury. After several X-rays and rehab discussions, both Dr. von Stade and her assistant Karen felt water therapy would be best for my shoulder and easy enough on my back. Four weeks of treading water and swimming in the deep end beneath the diving board at the Glenwood Hot Springs Pool really helped. I looked at that diving board and said, "It's just a matter of time until I will be as good as new and diving once again."

A month prior to my accident I thought this book was finished. I was fairly certain my ski career was over, although deep down I didn't want it to end. As I continued my water therapy, which by now allowed me enough mobility to attempt a lazy breaststroke and an adequate backstroke, I decided that the diving board was next, at least to jump.

I had weekly check-up and X-ray appointments with Dr. Lee Lee von Stade, who by now I called Lee Lee. It was my understanding that not having my humerus plated and screwed at the time of the accident was reason for concern. On my most recent visit, Lee Lee scrutinized my X-ray, scratched her head and asked me if I had ever had a bone density test. I told her I had one several years back and had been prescribed osteoporosis medication. Lee Lee discussed the possibility of brittle bone disease, all of which was a little confusing to me. My only experience with osteoporosis was with my mom who suffered from it early on in her life. Her ankles and thumbs had been fused, which limited her daily activities. Later on she suffered from multiple fractures, which eventually crippled her.

As I was leaving Lee Lee's office scratching my head as I did most of the time, I thought I'd better drop off a note to my primary physician Dr. Susan

Inscore letting her know what had just transpired. I wasn't sure if Lee Lee and Susan were communicating. Now with the mention of a bone density test and additional blood work, I felt the time had come.

Just a few days passed when I received a call from Carla Susan's assistant telling me Dr. Inscore needed to see me ASAP. In her office, she explained that she wanted to switch my osteoporosis medication from an oral to an injectable, which had to be administered at her office. She began talking with me in-depth about my medical history — mainly bone-related.

Susan had been my doctor since she first came to Glenwood Springs, about 20 years prior. She knew my medical history better than I did, however, now she seemed to be digging deeper. I felt so grateful for our lengthy doctor-patient relationship and how earnestly she kept up with my medical history. I was just now beginning to understand why all of this was an imperative.

As I was leaving Susan's office en route to Glenwood for pool therapy, my head was spinning over my discussion with Lee Lee the week prior. We had talked about my arm, the sacral fractures, bone density, blood work, and the possibility of a tumor. Now having just left Susan's office, the words "osteoporosis", "low testosterone", and "wasting disease" were steadily increasing my anxiety. I decided to do some research on the Internet. I didn't like the sound of wasting disease.

At the pool, I grabbed my coffee and newspaper. Wondering if everything happened for a reason, would I get some sort of hint from God? Having been dealing with this for two months, I was still uncertain when the light at the end of the tunnel would appear. I've had two near-death experiences and though it's a cliché, my whole life really did flash in front of me. As I was treading water, I recalled the last time it had happened. Rather than everything zooming right by me, it actually seemed to have happened quite slowly.

Reflecting on my past helps me understand why all this has happened. I honestly think that to get through the hoops life throws at us that one has to cheat. It's only human nature and maybe in my case, those hoops aren't coming at me as fast as I thought. If they came one at a time, I might be able to figure it out and get right through it; but they come in twos and threes, one right after the other. By the time I get through them, my thoughts lean more toward "whew". In most cases, I never do take the time to figure out just how I did get through those hoops. If next time I pause to reflect, it might be easier.

I was watching a lifeguard with great flipping skills go off the diving board. Tall and lanky with the perfect swimmer's body, Ryan was able to get huge air and was fun to watch. After a couple of days observing him and his buddies perform half pipe air tricks in preparation for the upcoming snowboard season, I got INSPIRED!

By now everyone at the pool knew that in my youth I had placed fourth in the City of Los Angeles Springboard Diving competition. Chance, another lifeguard, had Googled me and found my world record certificate, Rossignol poster, and assorted photos that *Vintage Ski World* sold. I imagined in the back of their minds they were thinking that I was nuts. That I may have been good in my day, but come on — "Tommy was getting up there and how long could he live in the past?"

A couple of days later, I arrived early at the pool. It was a beautiful morning. The pool opened at 7:30 a.m. and I liked going early to finish my therapy before the crowds arrived. I generally would stay just long enough to watch the kids play on the diving board. Today I wanted to jump off of it. Lee Lee had warned me, "Just don't dive." With that in mind I walked up the ladder onto the platform, thinking that the board wasn't all that wide. Feeling scared, maybe all I could do was jump, and questioned if I even wanted to do that. When I reached the end of the board, looking down at the water, I felt as though I were on a three-meter springboard ten feet high. In reality, I was only three feet from the water. I gently bounced a couple of times then jumped. Fortunately, nothing hurt other than my pride. I returned to the board and gave it another try. This time my approach included two steps and a small hurdle. Oops! As I hit the water, I felt every vertebrae in my thoracic spine crack and re-adjust. I could only hope that everything was all right, but I wouldn't know for a few hours.

The next day, I realized things weren't okay. Luckily, I had an appointment scheduled with Lee Lee the following day, but I'd be damned if I told her what I had done. Besides, I really didn't want to know if I had caused further damage.

When I did see her, although the word "tumor" was never mentioned, she still seemed puzzled over how I could have broken a bone in my sacrum. It was highly unusual for someone to do that… unless you were Evel Knievel. Great! Only Evel and I could. Hardly a compliment, but I'll take it. I always have related to being "a little crazy."

Despite everything, I was feeling better by now. Susan had started me on testosterone injections, administered every two weeks in her office. I didn't think I needed them. I had tried a topical 10 years ago for about a year, but hadn't like it. It made me itch and feel a bit scared. Not noticing a positive change, I had stopped taking it. This time, Susan told me that it would it make me feel better and keep me from breaking any more bones. The first words out of my mouth were, "Where do I sign?" If I was going to feel better and not have to worry about more fractures, all I could think was, "Look out."

Tracy and Maxwell arrived for the summer. For me it couldn't have come soon enough. I was so therapied out and needed a break from the whole rehab deal. It gave me a chance to play with Maxwell and his buddies who had come along. Stan and Tracy rented an absolutely beautiful home for the summer. Situated on 25 acres, her place overlooked McLain Flats with views from Independence Pass to Mt. Sopris. For the kids it was an ideal playground filled with ponds, horses, elk, a pool, trampoline, and a full gym that they could only use under my supervision. Seeing them do flips on the tramp and in the pool was like watching a chip off the old block. I had a blast being part of their audience, but it was a challenge keeping them safe. I got a real kick out of all the drama they created. Austin was Maxwell's best friend, Aiden was Austin's little brother. Despite Maxwell and Austin being older and bigger, Aiden was the best flipper, outclassing them with finesse. Yet they never failed to beat him up and I loved it. It was so "boys".

While Maxwell was in town, I did more PT out of the pool. I started hiking more and spending time strengthening my core. As my arm improved, I realized that over the last couple of years having sustained a hip fracture, broken femur, and now sacral fractures, if I was ever going to dive again, my core needed to get a lot stronger. After Maxwell left, I started spending more time at the pool. It was about the only thing, besides hiking, that I enjoyed doing. Both activities really helped clear my head.

I've thought a lot about my mom and my career with Ed. I feel really lucky to being living my life as it is and has been. I wouldn't change it for anything. At the same time, I'm uncertain why all this has happened. I know I'm not done yet, there's one more something in me. I just don't know what it is. I feel like that axiom, "A body in motion tends to stay in motion, while a body at rest tends to stay at rest." I find myself on a mission once again to try everything I can to make something good out of something bad. When I think back to December 2010, I had three major accidents along with two D.U.I.s that were eventually dismissed, thank God. It has taken until now to get out from under that dark cloud. Now I am ready to do something.

When they were good little boys. 2007

Tommy's Flying Circus Is Born

It's a beautiful fall Saturday morning and the colors are changing in the hills around Glenwood. With the kids back in school, the pool is in the hands of those who soak religiously to get the healing effect of the hot mineral spring water — the same qualities that have brought people here since the late 1800s. When the diving area had been as busy as it had ever been, it was amazing to watch those kids, some of whom had been first-timers on the diving board. Noticing a dad in the water trying to instill enough confidence in his child to jump, it had reminded me of my mom bribing me to jump off the board when I was nine. I recall the diving shows her boyfriends had taken me to as an inspiration.

Then it hit me. I would take everything I'd learned from Cush 'n' Carry, The World Kindness campaign, and Tommy's Magic Sauces. Loops for Lupus would be moved from slope side to poolside and called "Tommy's Flying Circus." I could achieve another world record and create a fundraising tool to help kids deal with adversity through support, compassion, and confidence.

With crystal clear vision, I understood my mission. Not only could I see what I wanted, now I could envision each step to get me there as I had done with Loops for Lupus. It was just like the experience I had had as a boy, attempting to find the hidden pictures in the children's magazine *Highlights*. Before I saw the picture, I'd already found 80% of the hidden gems. My

Diving with future circus clowns clones!

I had to try knowing Lee Lee could fix it tomorrow. 2013

Lost in space! 2013

brain only cared about not failing and didn't see the whole picture until later. My brother Willie used to tell me I was weird, and not to tell anyone, but I thought it was quite an accomplishment to beat him at something.

Although I don't have to get back on the diving board to put Tommy's Flying Circus together, if Guinness will allow me to establish another record, the talented young divers I attract will someday break them. Maybe someone will even break my record doing flips on skis.

Just Fix It

Things weren't feeling totally right and Lee Lee wanted me to have another CAT scan of my entire upper arm and shoulder to determine what may be going on. Although I could read an X-ray, I couldn't read an MRI or CAT scan. To me it looked like the inside of a fish. I needed Lee Lee's expertise to navigate me through it. As it turned out, the CAT scan revealed that although my humerus had fought to heal, with the entire trauma my body had been through it hadn't known what part to focus on. The bottom line: it hadn't healed. The ball had moved and created its own socket within the shoulder socket. I told Lee Lee, "Just fix it!"

We went ahead and scheduled the surgery, not knowing what to expect until she got in there. She decided to wait and reschedule until she had all her tools in place. The delay didn't bother me. I was so spent physically, I was at the point where I'd do anything just to be done with it all.

I kept up with my hiking and swimming. Not only did it continue to help me emotionally, I figured the better shape I was in before surgery the better and faster my recovery would be. Maybe I could do a flip before my surgery. What did I have to lose?

The only thing going through my mind as they wheeled me in for surgery was to please spare me from any complications, so I can pull off "Tommy's Flying Circus." It was time for that puppy to get back in the pickup; in other words here comes the anesthesia. As I woke up in recovery, Lee Lee was there looking over me. I asked her what she had done with my shoulder and she answered, "Nothing."

Once she had gotten the plate and screws in place (which was no easy task), she saw that the humerus was lined up perfectly in my shoulder socket.

"So that's good right?"

"Yeah we got lucky." As she was leaving my curtain-clad room she turned and asked me, "What's Tommy's Flying Circus?"

I winked and said, "I can't wait to tell you all about it."

Retrospect

I suppose I've had the opportunity to be wealthy. Successful in a variety of endeavors, I wanted to experiment in life, try different things and explore what life had to offer. Money was never the driving force. When you've gone full circle rags to riches and back to rags as I have, hopefully you learn that receiving is easy… giving without expectation is hard. Remembering that success isn't measured in wealth rather the journey and the quality and quantity of friends and friendships you've made along the way.

Wow! I could never be as big in my career as some of the friends I've made along the way. But our journeys together have truly been an inspiration to me and everyone they've touched. I feel so grateful to have been a part of it. —Tommy

Klaus Obermeyer adding his signature to my Loops for Lupus "Mango" suit, to be donated to the Aspen Historical Society. 2015

Acknowledgments

There is no way I could possibly thank everyone
who helped me along the way. My journey was colorful to say the
least.
I wrote my memoir exactly the way I remember it and the way I
wish to remember it. In the opening paragraph of "About My Story,"
my mom wanted me to write a book about my ski career and that's
what I've done. As far as reading it, why start now? I was afraid I
might change it!

I sincerely wish to thank;

Michael Morgan, George Mckerrow, Kyle Rost
Greg "Wolfy" Smith, Scott Wheeler, Dale Potvin, Tracy Shopkorn,
John Douglas, Bob Snow, Joe Kittinger, Dave Jensen,
Willie Waltner, Chris Hanson

Ski School Directors
Bill Sim, June Mountain, California
Curt Chase, Jan Johansen, Aspen, Colorado

Photographers
John Russell, Grafton Smith, John Hunt

Sponsors
Rossignol Ski Co., Volkl - Technica, Obermeyer Skiwear,
Aspen Skiing Company, Long Horn Steaks

Editors
Maggie Mcvoy, Amy Krakow
Copy Editor Stephanie Manone

Design
Basalt Printing

Scanning & Photo Work
Howard Freeman/Slidemaster, Aspen, Colorado

Diving with Angels

EVOLUTION OF

Tommy's Flying Circus™ Leadership Academy

Giving kids a chance to be the best they can today
for a better tomorrow.

CONFIDENCE **COMMITMENT** **INTEGRITY**

Courtesy Rhonda Foley 2014

REACH **ACHIEVE** **SUCCEED**

If I could do it, so can you!

*Had I known, when this accident happened, that the diving board was
going to become the driving force to my recovery and that I was going
to be able to do this dive, a dive I haven't attempted in 15 years,
the journey would have been that much sweeter!*

For questions and comments
visit
skiingismypassion.com
or TommyWaltner.com

Images in this book available online at
skiingismypassion.com

Discounts available for:
non-profits, fundraising, corporations and quantities.

Happy
Trails